my first book of animals

Published by arrangement with
Weldon Owen Pty Ltd
59–61 Victoria Street, McMahons Point
Sydney NSW 2060, Australia

WELDON OWEN PTY LTD
Chief Executive Officer Sheena Coupe
Creative Director Sue Burk
Publisher Corinne Roberts
Senior Vice President, International Sales Stuart Laurence
Sales Manager, North America Ellen Towell
Vice President Sales: Asia and Latin America Dawn L. Owen
Administration Manager, International Sales Kristine Ravn
Production Director Todd Rechner
Production Controller Lisa Conway
Publishing Coordinator Mike Crowton
Production Assistant Nathan Grice

Consultant Editor Denise Ryan
Managing Editor Jessica Cox
Editor Helen Flint
Editorial Assistant Hunnah Jessup
Designer Gabrielle Green
Cover Design Hilda Mendham

ISBN: 978-1-74252-080-3

Color reproduction by SC (Sang Choy) International Pte Ltd
Printed by Toppan Leefung Printing Ltd
Manufactured in China

A WELDON OWEN PRODUCTION

my first
book of animals

Robert Coupe

Helen Flint

Denise Ryan

contents

Fish

Scarlet macaws

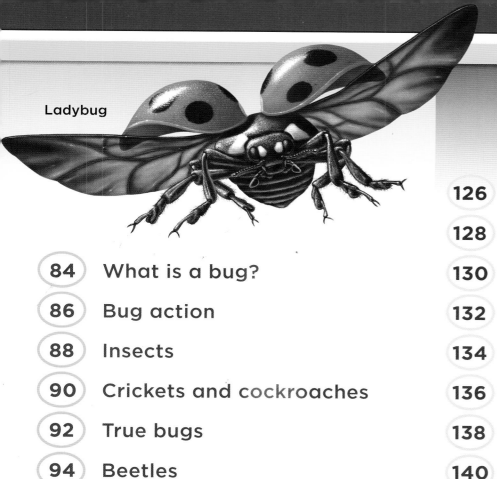
Ladybug

Monitor lizard

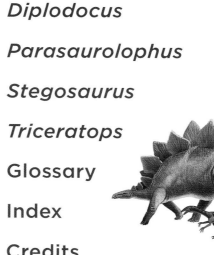

What is an animal?

Spiders, frogs, birds, and bears are all animals. Animals with backbones are called vertebrates. Elephants, bears, birds, sharks, and frogs are vertebrates. Animals without backbones are called invertebrates. Butterflies, ants, spiders, and worms are all invertebrates.

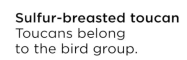

Sulfur-breasted toucan
Toucans belong to the bird group.

Brown bear
Bears belong to the mammal group.

What group?

Many animals are very similar to each other. Others are quite different. Animals that are similar are grouped together and given a group name.

Silvertip

The large, gray silvertip shark is a vertebrate because it has a backbone.

Silvertip shark
Sharks belong to the fish group.

Elephant
Elephants belong to the mammal group.

Tarantula
Tarantulas belong to the spider group.

Strawberry poison dart frog
Frogs belong to the amphibian group.

An elephant's trunk has 150,000 bands of muscle.

Kangaroos

Kangaroos are a kind of animal called marsupials. They live in the deserts and grasslands of Australia, where they eat plants. Kangaroos hop on their strong back legs. All female kangaroos have pouches where their babies shelter and feed on their mother's milk.

Boxing kangaroos

Male kangaroos look like they are boxing when they kick and push each other. The winner of the boxing match mates with a female kangaroo.

A male kangaroo is sometimes called a boomer.

Kangaroos live in family groups called mobs. They usually feed in the evening and rest during the day.

Platypus

Australian neighbors

Kangaroos live only in Australia. Two other animals that live only in Australia are the platypus and the echidna.

Ants

Echidna

Monkeys

There are almost 200 different kinds of monkeys. Monkeys live in Africa, Asia, and Central and South America. Some have tails that can grasp and hold objects. Others can grab objects with their fingers and toes. Monkeys live in family groups and spend most of their time in trees.

Woolly monkey

This woolly monkey uses its tail to grip tree branches. This allows it to collect food with its hands.

Hanging on

South American spider monkeys use their tails to hang onto slender branches as they swing from tree to tree.

Cotton-tops

Cotton-top tamarins live in Central America. They spend most of their lives high in the rain forest trees, eating fruit, leaves, and insects.

Hot bath

Japanese macaques survive cold temperatures by bathing in hot springs.

Apes

The group of animals called apes is made up of orangutans, gorillas, and two kinds of chimpanzees. Orangutans live on the islands of Sumatra and Borneo, Indonesia. Gorillas and chimpanzees are found only in Africa.

Orangutan

The people of Sumatra and Borneo call this gentle red ape *Orang Hutan*, which means "People of the Forest."

Gorilla family

Gorillas live in family groups. Each family is led by a large silverback male. He stands upright, roars, and slaps his chest to warn other males to stay away from his mates and children.

Many apes build nests each night in the tops of trees.

Silverback male

Wolves

Wolves are members of a group called dogs. They have keen sight, hearing, and smell, and have 42 strong, sharp teeth. Wolves are excellent hunters and hunt their prey in packs. They let each other know what is happening by howling loudly.

Wolf pack

A wolf pack is led by an adult male and female. The other members of the pack are their children.

Dinnertime

Wolves slowly sneak up on their victim in single file. When their prey tries to escape, the wolves rush to attack.

Red foxes are also dogs.
They can dig holes,
and often bury food
to eat later.

Bears

What do you picture when you think of a bear? Maybe you see a a fierce brown bear or maybe a polar bear? Many bears live in forests and in the icy Arctic. They all have heavy bodies, long, sharp claws, and huge heads with big teeth.

Meal time

Bears eat plants, insects, honey, as well as meat if they can catch it easily. This brown bear has found a marmot's burrow. If it can catch the marmot, it will eat it.

A polar bear's fur is made up of hollow hairs that trap heat. This helps it live in freezing Arctic areas.

Marmot

FUR PATTERN

The giant panda is mainly white. It has black fur on its ears, eye patches, muzzle, legs, and shoulders. It eats only bamboo.

Sharp claw

Some bears spend all winter in a deep sleep in their dens.

Lions

Lions are a member of the animal group called cats. They have fur, sharp teeth, and they work together to find food. Lions are the only cats to live in groups, which are called prides. Female lions, called lionesses, usually hunt for the whole pride.

Lioness

Lioness lunch

This lioness leaps quickly to grab its frightened prey, a gazelle. If she catches it, other lionesses and lions will join her for the meal.

A pride of lions

Lion prides usually have 4 to 6 animals, although they can have up to 30 members. The females are nearly always related to each other.

Lions can survive for long periods without water.

Lion cub

Tigers

Tigers are the largest members of the cat group. Tigers live in forests and grasslands of India, Siberia, and southeast Asia. They have powerful jaws filled with large teeth. Striped fur covers their bodies.

Even though lots of cats hate getting wet, tigers love water and are good swimmers.

FUR COAT

Tigers have thick black stripes covering their orange bodies. Male tigers have a ruff of fur around the back of their heads.

Stripy fur

The hunt

This tiger is creeping through tall grass to get close to its prey. When it is close enough, it pounces and catches its dinner.

White tigers are found only in zoos.

Elephants

The elephant is the largest living creature on land. The two kinds, the Indian and African elephants, live in family groups. Elephants are so big that they spend most of their time eating plants to fuel their bodies.

Elephants can make sounds that are too low for humans to hear.

Water, mud, and dust

African elephants stay cool by sucking water into their trunks and spraying it over their bodies. They also coat themselves with mud and dust to protect their skins from sunburn and insects.

Trunk
An elephant's trunk is sensitive enough to pick up a blade of grass.

DIFFERENCES

African elephants have large ears and a sloping forehead. Indian elephants have smaller ears and a domed forehead. Which one is the African elephant?

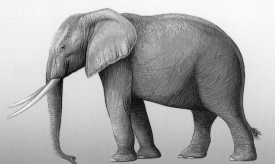 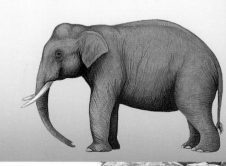

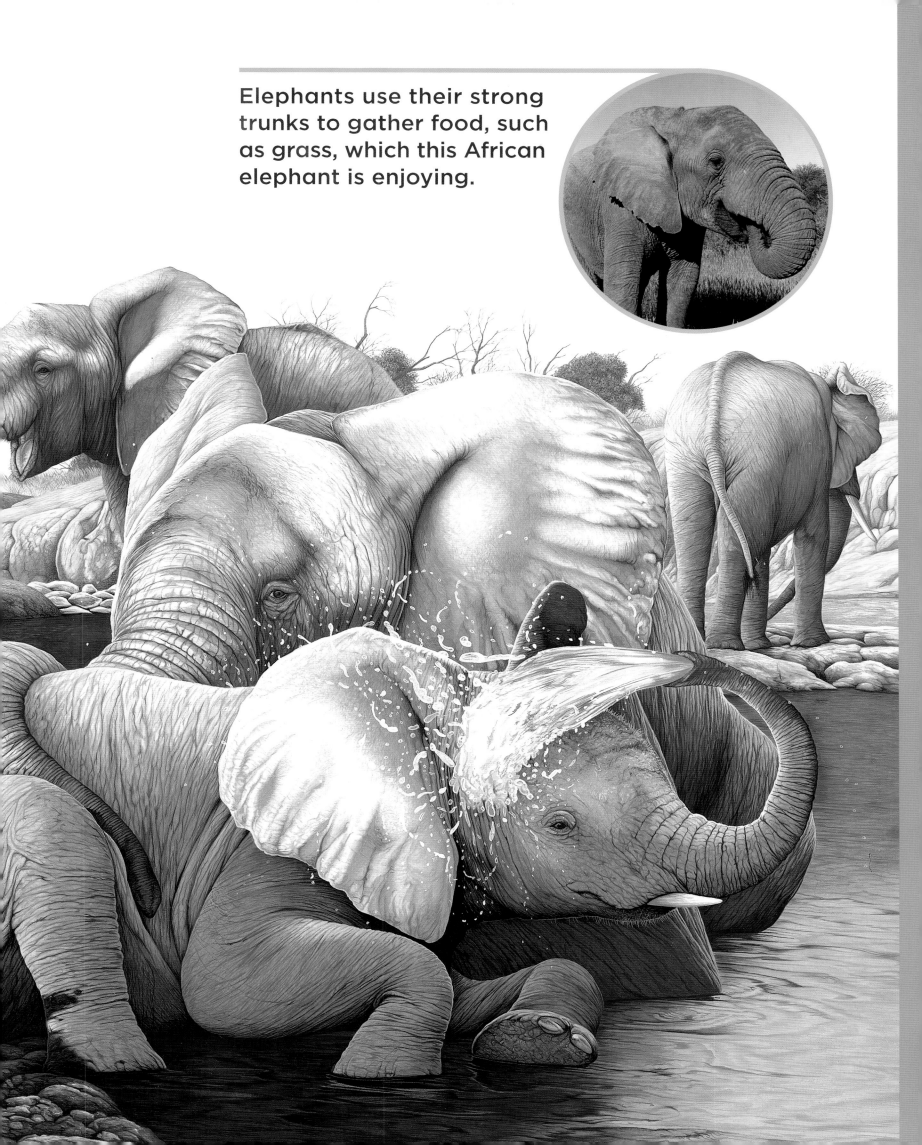

Elephants use their strong trunks to gather food, such as grass, which this African elephant is enjoying.

Rhinos

Rhinoceroses are large animals that live in Asia and Africa. Rhinos eat leaves, buds, shoots, and twigs. They drink freshwater every day, and spend a lot of time wallowing in waterholes to keep themselves cool. They have huge bodies, stumpy legs, and two horns.

Charge!

These spotted hyenas have no chance against a charging rhino. Rhinos usually defend themselves by attacking. They can run quickly when they need to!

Charging rhino

BODY TALK

When their young are under attack, female rhinos form a circle around them. They threaten the attacker with their horns.

Spotted hyena

Humans once hunted rhinos for their horns.

Whales

Whales are large mammals that live in the ocean. They breathe air through blowholes. Their sleek, streamlined bodies move easily through the water. They give birth to calves that can see and swim straight away.

Despite their size, orcas can leap clear out of the water. No one knows exactly why they do it.

DOLPHINS

Dolphins belong to the same group of animals as whales. There are 32 kinds of dolphins. Three of them are below.

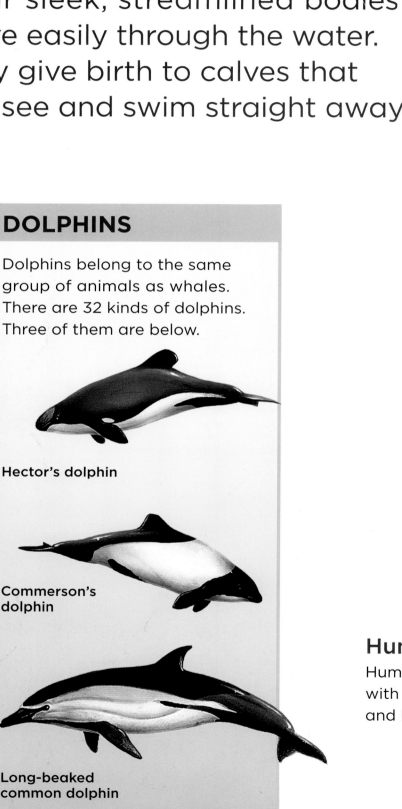

Hector's dolphin

Commerson's dolphin

Long-beaked common dolphin

Humpback whales

Humpback whales are a grayish-blue color with light spots. They have stubby dorsal fins and large, thick tails. They feed mainly on krill.

One bowhead whale was thought to have reached 130 years of age.

Giants of the sea

Whales are mammals, just like you and me. Female whales feed their babies on milk from their bodies. Whales have strong tails that they use to push themselves through the water. Many whales travel long distances across the world's oceans.

Baleen

Whale tails

Fish tails move from side to side. Whale tails move up and down. Some whales slap their tails on the surface of the sea.

Holding their breath

Whales rise to the surface to breathe air through a hole in their heads, called a blowhole. But they can stay under the water without breathing for a long time.

Orca

Gray whale

Gray whale

Blue whale

Sei whale

The blue whale is the biggest animal anywhere in the world.

Orca

Dolphins and porpoises

You may have seen dolphins doing tricks at the zoo, or swimming, leaping, and diving near a beach. There are almost 40 kinds of dolphins, and some of them grow very large. Porpoises are generally smaller than dolphins and there are only six known kinds.

Fins

Porpoises use their backfin to help them swim. The finless porpoise is the only porpoise that does not have a fin on its back.

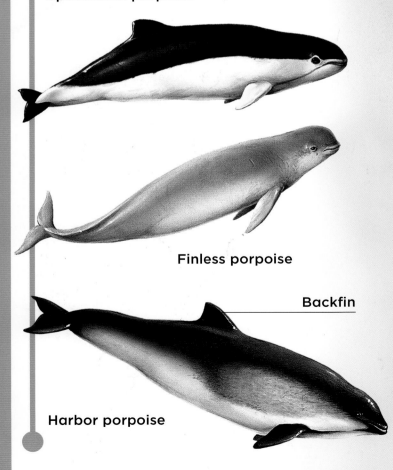

Spectacled porpoise

Finless porpoise

Backfin

Harbor porpoise

High jumps

Some dolphins jump high into the air. They do this when they are playing, but sometimes it is to tell other dolphins there are fish nearby.

Angry dolphins clap their jaws together and make whistling sounds.

Look alike

Dolphins that are closely related, like this mother and her calf, often look very much like each other.

Seals and sea lions

Adult sea lion

Seals are mammals, like whales and dolphins. However, seals spend much of their time on land and can move along the ground. Some seals have ears that you can see. They are sea lions. Other seals have ears that you cannot see.

Swimming for food

Sea lions, such as the ones here, swim in the sea to catch the fish and other sea creatures that they eat.

Flipper

Young sea lions can swim a month after they are born.

Fish

Pup

Tusks for digging

Walruses are close relatives of seals. They use their long tusks to dig crabs and shellfish from between rocks.

Jungle birds

Birds have light feathers, strong bones, and powerful flying muscles. A large number of beautiful birds live in the jungle. Most of them spend all their lives among the trees. The birds feed on insects, fruit, and seeds, and build nests high up in the branches.

Toucan

Toucans live in South American rain forests, where they use their colorful bills to pluck fruit, nuts, and berries from trees.

LONG LIFE

Parrots can live for a long time. This black-capped lory can live for more than 40 years.

Bill
A toucan's bill can be as big as its body.

Some toucans have bills almost half as long as their bodies.

Body talk
Scarlet macaws have wide, strong wings that help them to fly quickly. They often fly in pairs or small groups, and call to each other in loud voices.

Eagles

Eagles are some of the largest birds in the world. They can be found everywhere except Antarctica. They belong to a group called birds of prey, or raptors. Eagles are good at flying, have excellent vision, and have strong grasping talons, which makes them great hunters.

Feathered, not bald
Bald eagles are magnificent birds found in North America. They are large birds that have white heads and tails, and are not bald at all.

Spotted harrier
Spotted harriers fly low over fields, swooping down on any mice, frogs, lizards, and snakes they see.

Golden eagles are great hunters. They live in the rocky areas and mountains of North America.

About half of the world's 70,000 bald eagles live in Alaska, USA.

Wing

Owls

Owls sleep during the day and hunt at night. They have talons on their feet for catching prey and hooked beaks for tearing food apart. Their big eyes face forward and their large heads can swivel almost fully around.

A barn owl's eggs hatch after 33 days. The male helps feed the young chicks, which can fly after about 12 weeks.

Caught

Sometimes owls can be spotted hunting during the day, especially when they have young to feed. They mostly hunt small mammals.

Barn owl

The barn owl's large heart-shaped face, white breast, and pale golden wings can make it look quite ghostly at night.

Eye

Barn owls do not hoot. They screech, hiss, snore, and yap.

Penguins

Penguins are birds that do not fly. But they are good swimmers and divers. Most of them live in the cold southern parts of the world. Some penguins spend most of the time in the water. They hunt for fish and other sea animals.

Penguin diving

The smallest penguin, the little penguin, is smaller than a chicken.

Diving deep

Penguins can dive deep under the water. When they swim, they flap their wings, just like birds that fly in the air.

King penguin

Emperor penguins

Emperor penguins are the largest penguins of all. They grow to 4 feet (1.2 m) in height. They live in Antarctica all year round.

Snares penguin

Snares penguins live on a small island off the south coast of New Zealand. They have a small white patch on each cheek.

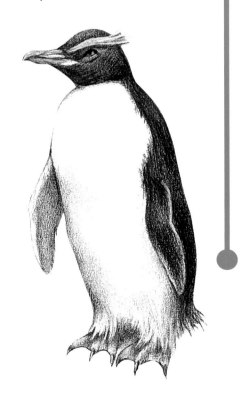

What is a sea creature?

Some animals, such as whales and many fish, spend all their lives in the sea. Some fish, such as salmon, move between seas and rivers. Other animals, such as penguins and seals, live on land but find their food in the sea. All these animals are sea creatures.

At home
Seals can swim in the sea and move on land.

Pineapple fish

Butterfly fish

Sea anemone

Organ pipe coral

All shapes and sizes

Creatures of all shapes and sizes live in the sea. Gray reef sharks swim and hunt in the open ocean, while brightly colored small fish live among coral reefs.

There are more than 24,000 different kinds of fish.

Octopus

Fish

Fish live in all the world's seas. They range from huge sharks to tiny creatures less than half-an-inch long. They have scales on their bodies, and use their side and tail fins to move through the water. They breathe through gills on the sides of their heads.

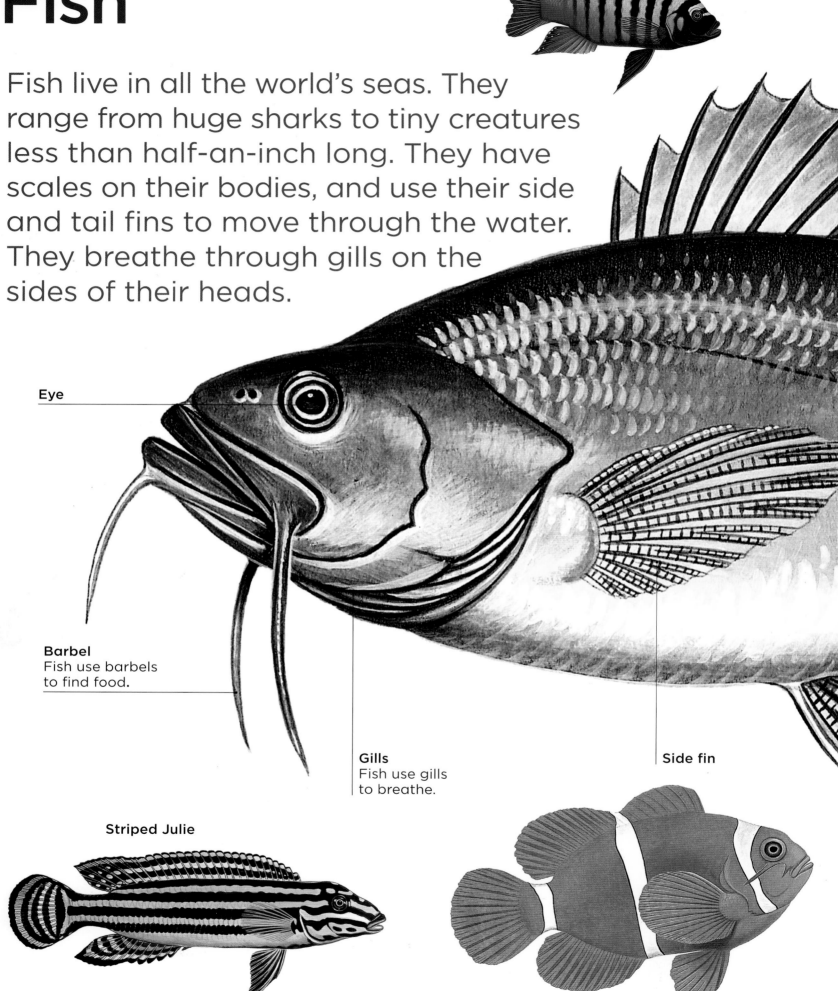

Malawi fish

Eye

Barbel
Fish use barbels to find food.

Gills
Fish use gills to breathe.

Side fin

Striped Julie

Spinecheek anemone fish

Light and dark

The top of many fish is darker than the bottom. This makes them harder to see and protects them from being attacked.

Top fin

All fish have black eyes.

Tail fin

Scaly skin

Puffer fish

Oscar fish

Sharks

There are about 350 kinds of sharks. All of them eat other fish and other sea creatures, but most will not harm humans. Many sharks use their strong tails to move quickly through the water. The whale shark can grow to 40 feet (12 m) in length and is the largest of all sharks.

INTO THE SEA

People who study great white and other dangerous sharks sometimes go under the sea in strong metal cages that the sharks cannot bite through.

Cage
Sharks cannot bite through the cage.

Shark

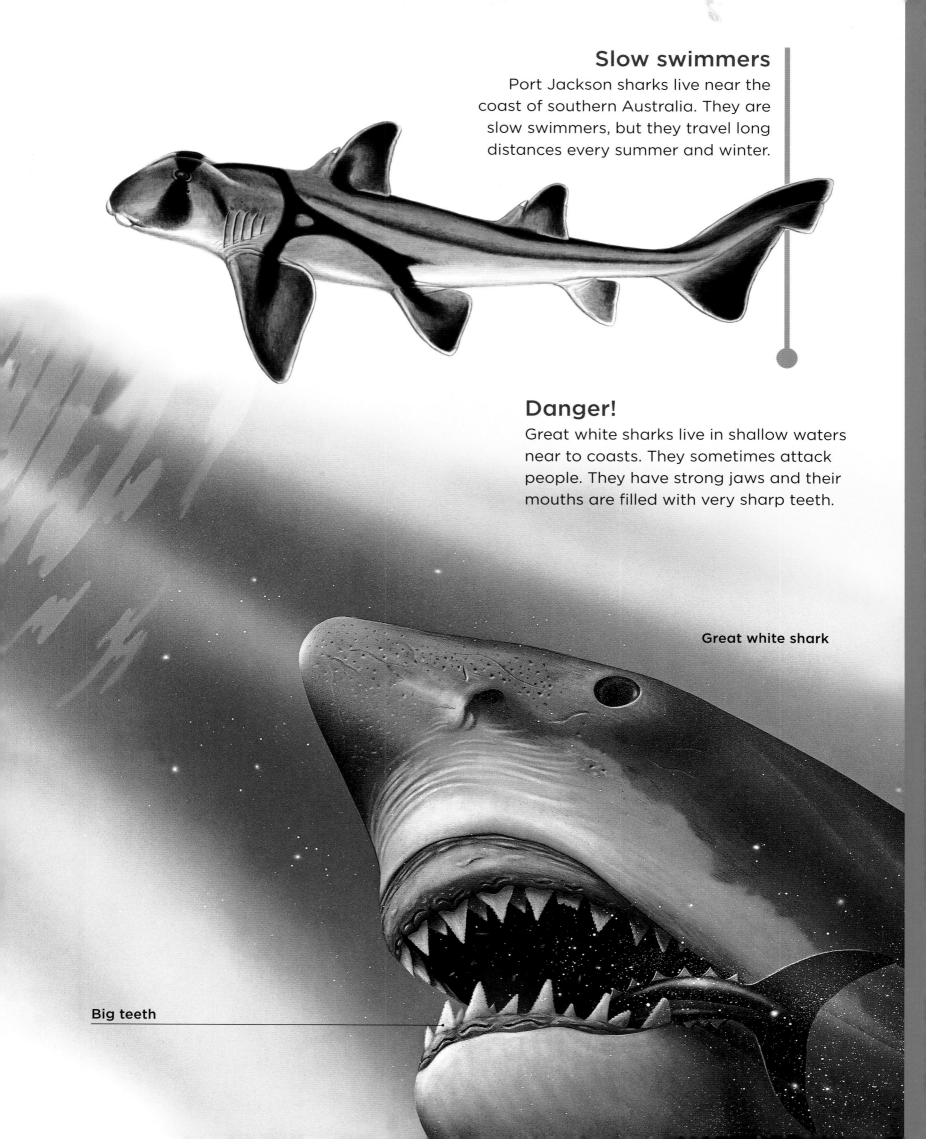

Slow swimmers

Port Jackson sharks live near the coast of southern Australia. They are slow swimmers, but they travel long distances every summer and winter.

Danger!

Great white sharks live in shallow waters near to coasts. They sometimes attack people. They have strong jaws and their mouths are filled with very sharp teeth.

Great white shark

Big teeth

Hunters

Sharks are amazing fish that live in every ocean around the world. They have sleek bodies that glide easily through the water. They attack their prey with their sharp teeth. Most sharks do not chew their food. They just gulp it down in large pieces.

Hammerhead sharks are fierce hunters with a good sense of smell for finding their prey.

SHARP AND DEADLY

Shark teeth come in many shapes and sizes. Different teeth are used for catching and eating different food.

Blue shark

Shortfin mako shark

Tiger shark

Great white shark

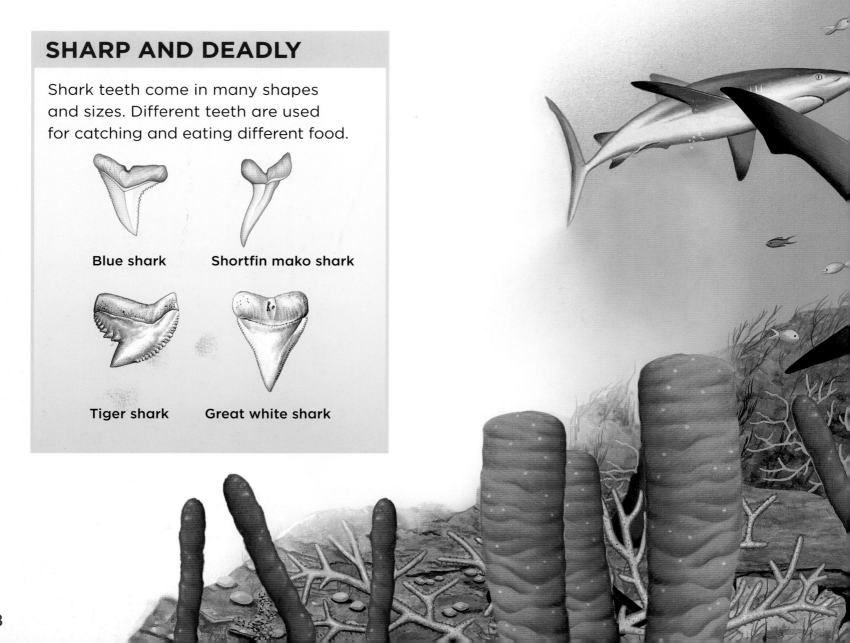

On the reef

Caribbean reef sharks live in tropical waters near the edge of coral reefs. They are found in the Caribbean Sea.

A shark may have up to 3,000 teeth in its mouth at one time.

Caribbean reef shark

Rays

Rays are fish that are close relatives of sharks. Their bodies are wide and flat and they have long, thin tails. They all have side fins that look similar to the wings of bats. There are six main types of rays.

When rays swim, they flap their side fins like the wings of a bird.

A sting in its tail

This stingray may look friendly, but a long spike at the tip of its tail can give a poisonous sting.

Electric fish

Torpedo rays catch the fish they eat by giving them an electric shock. They have organs behind their eyes that make electricity.

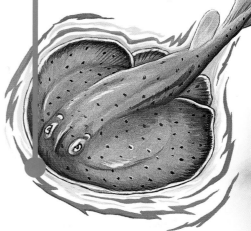

TWO FACES

A ray may seem to have two faces. Its eyes are on top of its head and its mouth and nostrils are underneath.

Nostril

Mouth

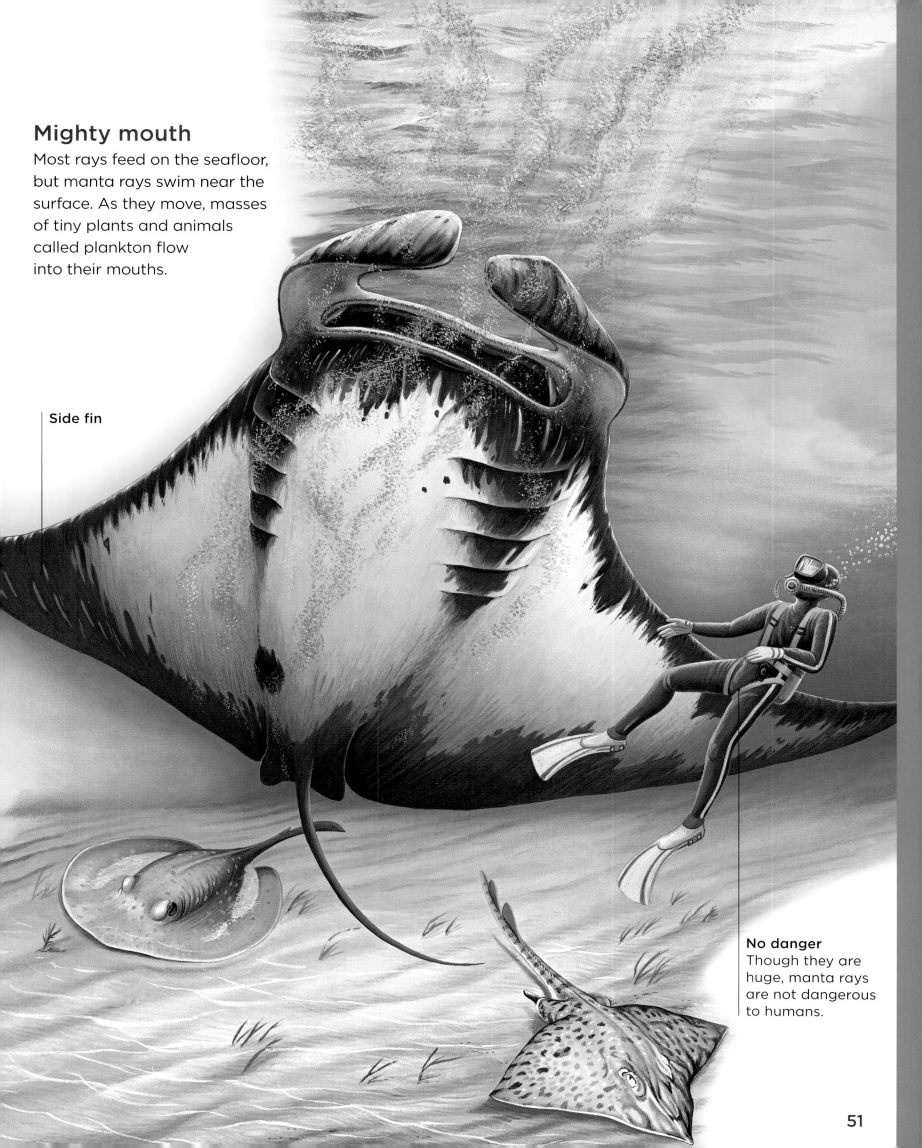

Mighty mouth

Most rays feed on the seafloor, but manta rays swim near the surface. As they move, masses of tiny plants and animals called plankton flow into their mouths.

Side fin

No danger
Though they are huge, manta rays are not dangerous to humans.

Octopuses and squid

Octopuses have eight arms, called tentacles. There are suckers on the tentacles that catch food. Squid are like octopuses. They have ten arms, which also have suckers for catching food. Some squid and octopuses are tiny. Some are huge.

Tiny but dangerous

The blue-ringed octopus is only as big as a golf ball, but it is highly poisonous.

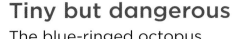

COLOR CHANGE

An octopus can change color quickly. It can make itself look like part of a rock or like sand.

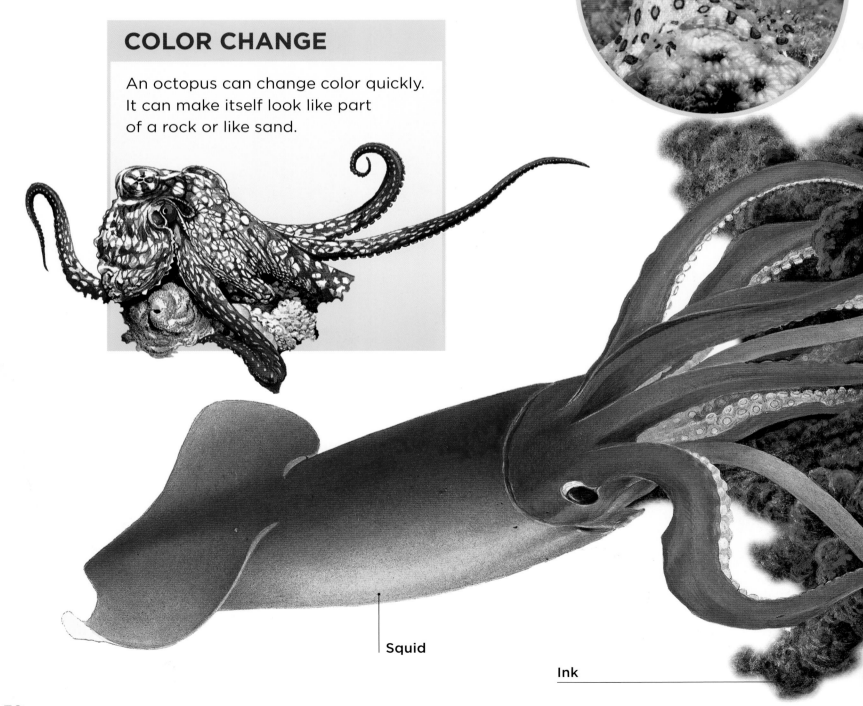

Squid

Ink

52

Squirting ink

When a shark or other animal attacks a squid, the squid can squirt a cloud of black ink from inside its body.

Frill shark

The giant squid can grow to the size of a bus.

Jewels of the sea

Many sea creatures live deep in the ocean where it is too dark to see any color. But in the warm, shallow waters of tropical areas, colorful coral reefs grow like huge underwater gardens. Brightly colored fish, shellfish, turtles, worms, and other creatures live among coral reefs.

Sea stars

We sometimes call sea stars starfish, but they are not fish. They have soft bodies and five arms that stick out like the points of a star.

SHELL HOMES

Many small sea creatures have shells that cover their bodies and help protect them from other animals.

Coral reefs

Most coral reefs are in the Pacific and Indian oceans. More than 3,000 different types of fish live on reefs in the Indian Ocean.

Coral reefs are the skeletons of small sea animals.

Jellyfish

The bodies of jellyfish look like bells. Underneath they have long arms, or tentacles, which they use to catch small animals.

Near the surface

Plankton is the name we use for the millions of tiny animals and plants that float in the sunlight on the sea's surface. Small fish and other small sea animals feed on plankton. Salmon and other larger fish then eat the small fish.

Hunters and hunted

An orca, or killer whale, chases a seal, while a salmon swims after a school of herring not far below the sea's surface.

Young salmon live in rivers. Adult salmon swim to the sea.

On coral reefs

Large schools of squirrelfish swim through coral reefs in the shallow tropical waters of the Pacific and Indian oceans.

IN AND OUT

Turtles can live in and out of the water. Many lobsters spend their lives under the water, in shallow coastal seas.

Turtle

Lobster

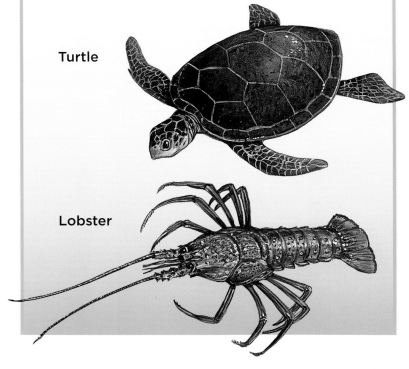

In the deep

Deep down in the sea, where the sunlight does not reach, it is very dark. Many sea creatures such as fish, squid, eels, and jellyfish, spend their lives in the ocean depths. Most deep-sea creatures never come to the surface.

Submarine

A big gulp
This black gulper eel has huge jaws, very small teeth, a tiny eye, and a long tail that gets thinner and thinner toward the end.

Hatchet fish

Gulper eel

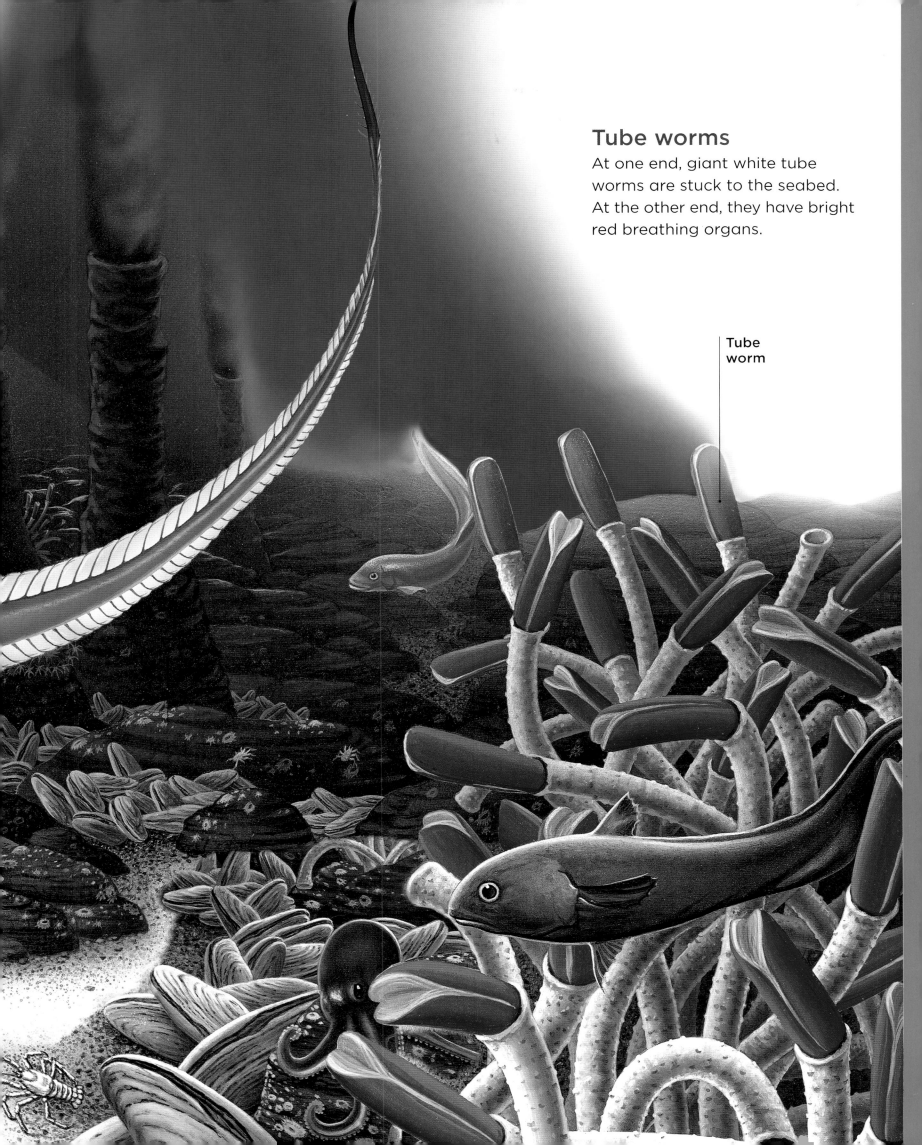

Tube worms

At one end, giant white tube worms are stuck to the seabed. At the other end, they have bright red breathing organs.

Tube worm

Big and small

The world's biggest animal, the blue whale, lives in the sea. So do plankton, which are some of the world's tiniest creatures. Plankton are so small you cannot see them. They are the main food for some of the largest whales and sharks.

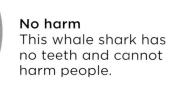

No harm
This whale shark has no teeth and cannot harm people.

Whale shark

Big fish

The whale shark is not only the biggest of all sharks; it is also the biggest of all fish. It feeds mainly on plankton and small fish.

Great white shark

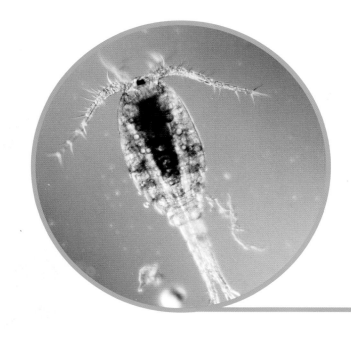

Krill are tiny sea creatures that look like shrimp. Many whales, seals, and seabirds eat krill.

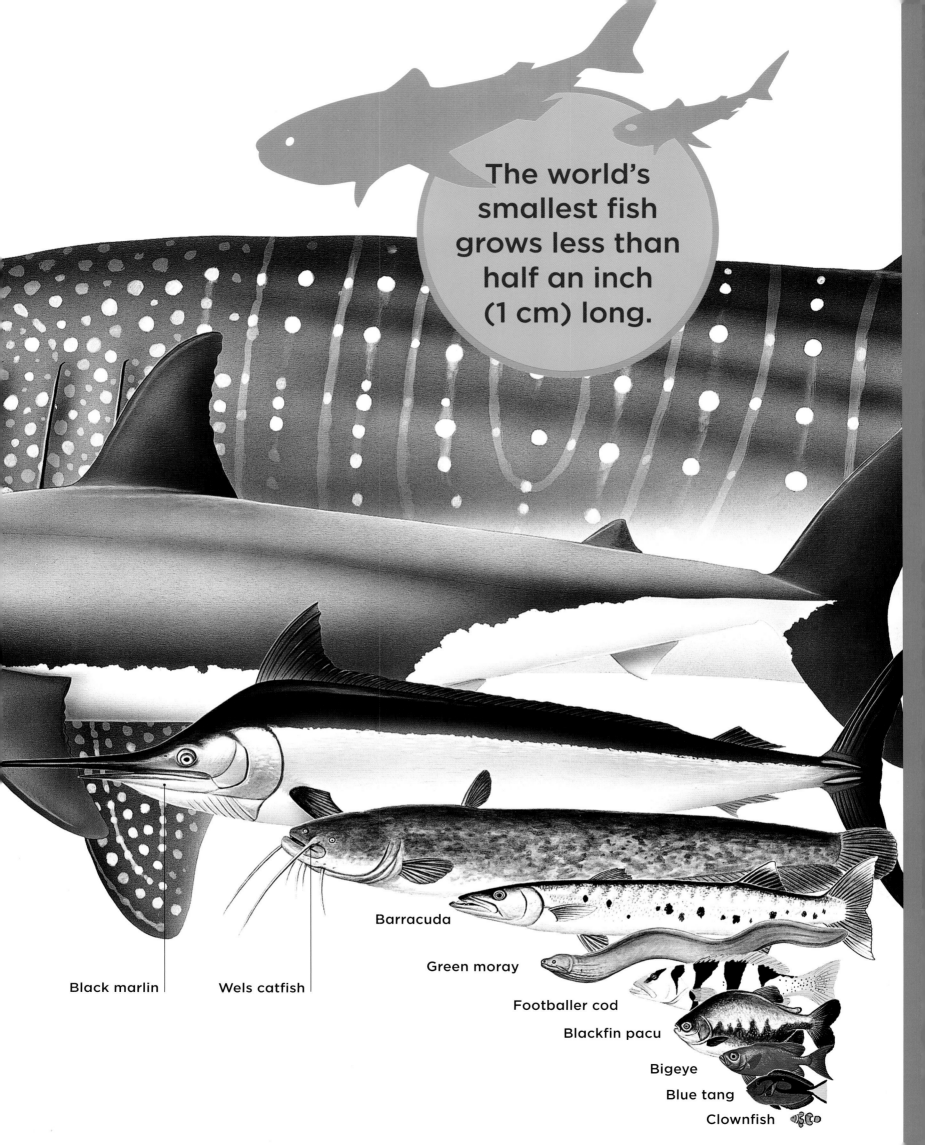

The world's smallest fish grows less than half an inch (1 cm) long.

Barracuda

Green moray

Black marlin

Wels catfish

Footballer cod

Blackfin pacu

Bigeye

Blue tang

Clownfish

Great hunters

Most sea creatures hunt other animals. Some eat only one kind of fish or animal. Others eat different types of food. In most cases, larger animals hunt for smaller animals. Some animals hunt alone. Others search for food in groups or in large packs.

The orca is one of the fastest creatures in the sea.

Deadly tail

The tail of the thresher shark is like a long whip. The shark uses its tail to trap fish and then beat them to death.

Tail

Killer whales

Orcas, or killer whales, are clever hunters. Sometimes an orca will lunge onto a beach and frighten seals into the water, where other orcas catch and eat them.

Protection

Different animals have different ways of protecting themselves against attack. Some fish have bright colors, stripes, or spots that make them hard to see. Other sea creatures have to fight back to save themselves from being caught and eaten.

Puffing up

Puffer fish can puff up their bodies until they are too large for other fish to swallow. Their bodies also contain a strong poison.

Circle of tails

Sperm whales form a circle around their young when orcas attack them. They slap the water hard with their tails to frighten the orcas away.

SWORD FIGHT

Narwhals are whales with long tusks that are similar to swords. Male narwhals use these tusks to defend themselves and to fight each other over females.

Clownfish live among the stinging tentacles of sea anemones to stay safe.

Next generation

Most baby fish hatch from eggs. At first they are tiny creatures, called larvae. They swim freely in the ocean until they grow into adults. Other sea creatures, such as whales, give birth to babies that are fully formed and ready to swim.

Mother humpback whale

FIRST BREATH

As soon as an Irrawaddy dolphin is born, its mother takes it to the surface to get its first breath of air.

Humpback calf

Mother and child

When it is born, a baby humpback whale is about one-third the size of its mother. It grows quickly by sucking milk from its mother's body.

All baby clownfish are born male. Some turn into females later in life.

Legends of the sea

In days gone by, long sea journeys were very dangerous. So it is not surprising that sailors made up stories featuring imaginary sea monsters. Some of these monsters are similar to sea creatures that really exist.

Kraken tentacle

Kraken

In Norway, people told stories about a creature similar to a giant octopus. It was called a kraken. It could hold a ship in its huge tentacles.

Scary beasts

The animals below are imaginary creatures. However, there are some real sea animals that look a bit like them.

Looking after the sea

The oceans are home to millions of sea creatures. However, people use the oceans, too. They swim in them, fish them, and sail ships across them. Some of the things that people do can harm the oceans and the creatures that live there.

Oil that spills from big ships can kill or injure sea animals, such as this sea otter.

Trapped by mistake

Fishing nets often catch the wrong kinds of sea animals. Dolphins and sharks that get caught in these nets can be injured or killed.

WHALE PRODUCTS

Whales were once killed for their oil. This oil was used for many things, including face creams and candles.

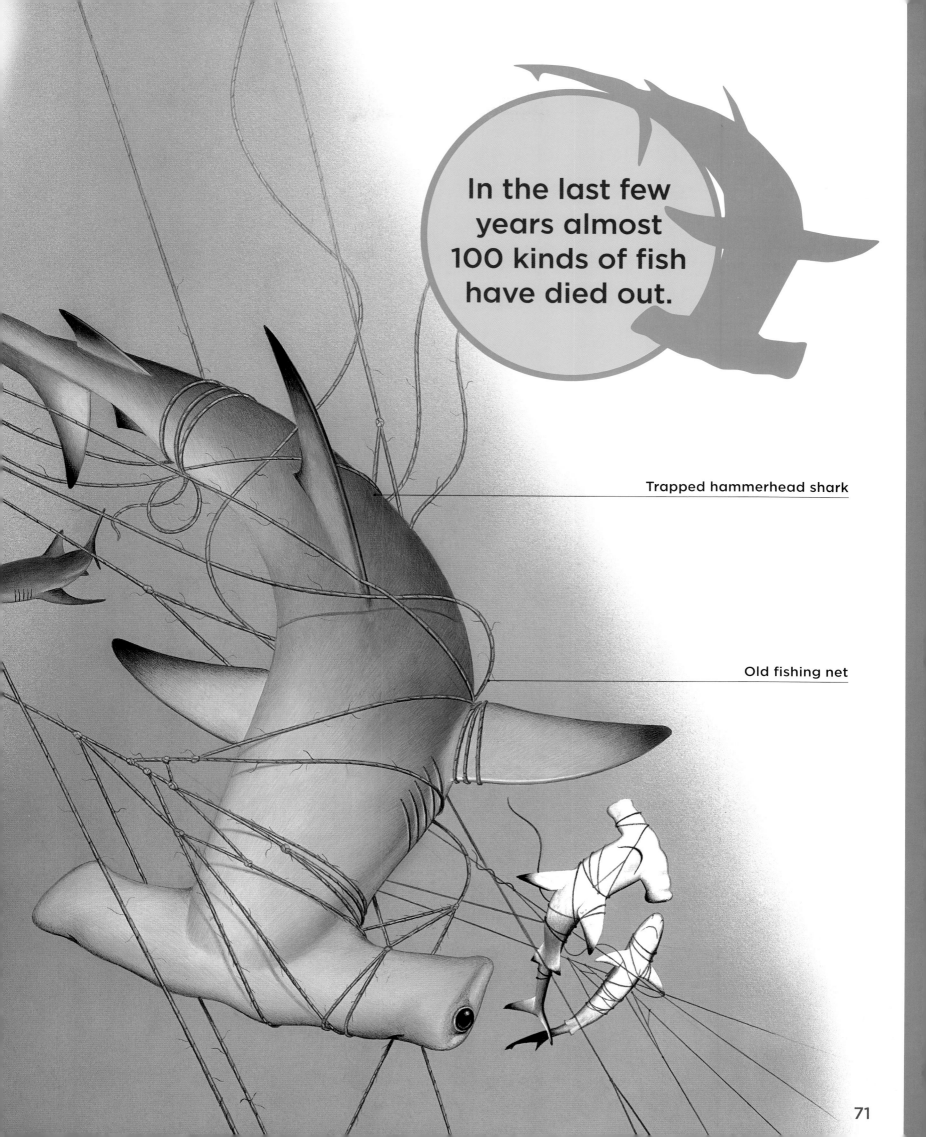

In the last few years almost 100 kinds of fish have died out.

Trapped hammerhead shark

Old fishing net

Crocodiles

Crocodiles and their close relatives, alligators, are large reptiles. They wait for prey to come to the water's edge, then use their strong teeth to drag it underwater. Crocodiles cannot chew, so they tear their food into chunks, which they swallow whole.

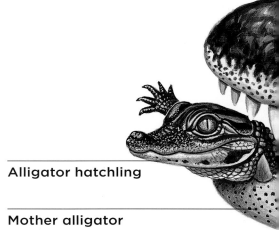

If a crocodile's tooth gets knocked out, another grows to take its place.

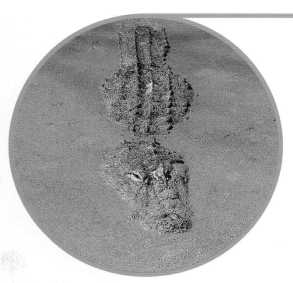

Hiding out
The alligator hides under the algae on the water's surface.

Alligator hatchling

Mother alligator

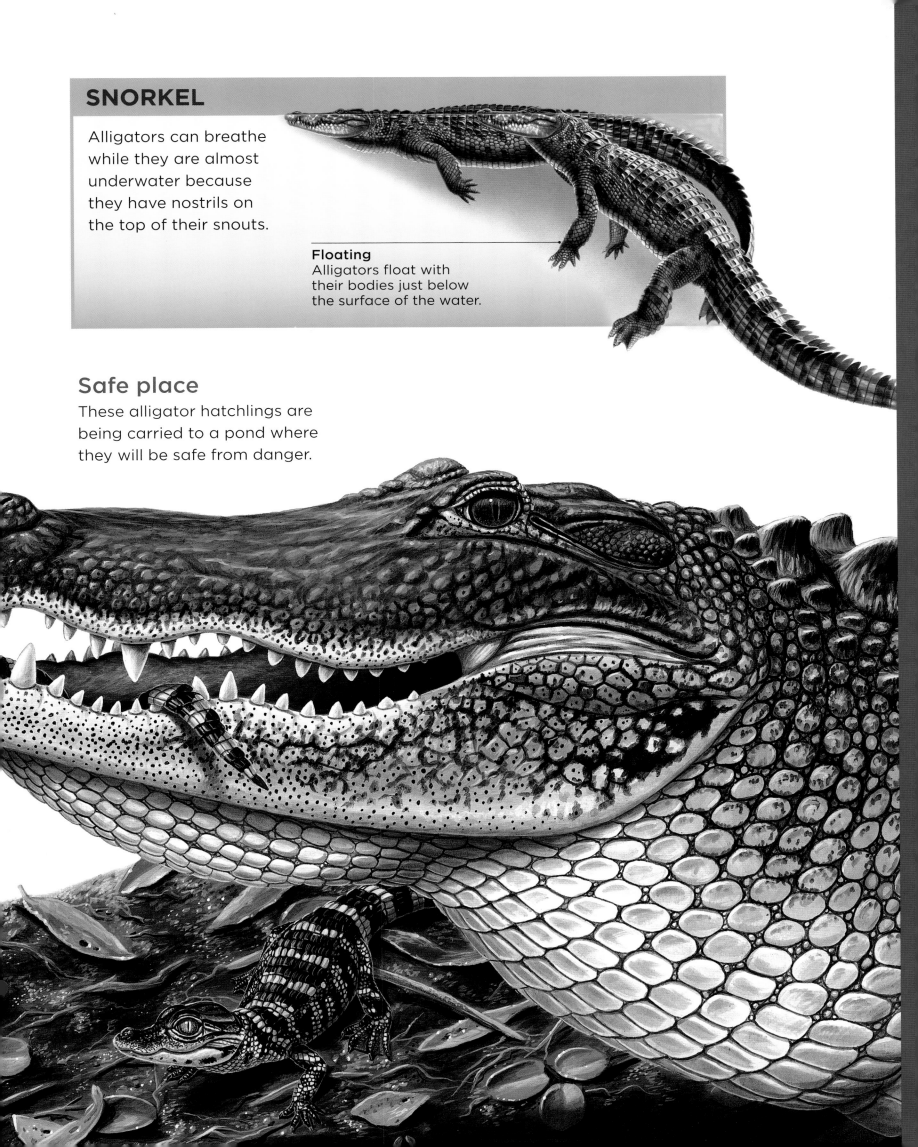

SNORKEL

Alligators can breathe while they are almost underwater because they have nostrils on the top of their snouts.

Floating
Alligators float with their bodies just below the surface of the water.

Safe place

These alligator hatchlings are being carried to a pond where they will be safe from danger.

Lizards

Lizards have many enemies, such as snakes and birds. Most lizards are able to blend into the background and stay completely still when an enemy approaches. Some lizards have an unusual way of escaping. If they are grabbed by the tail they leave it behind!

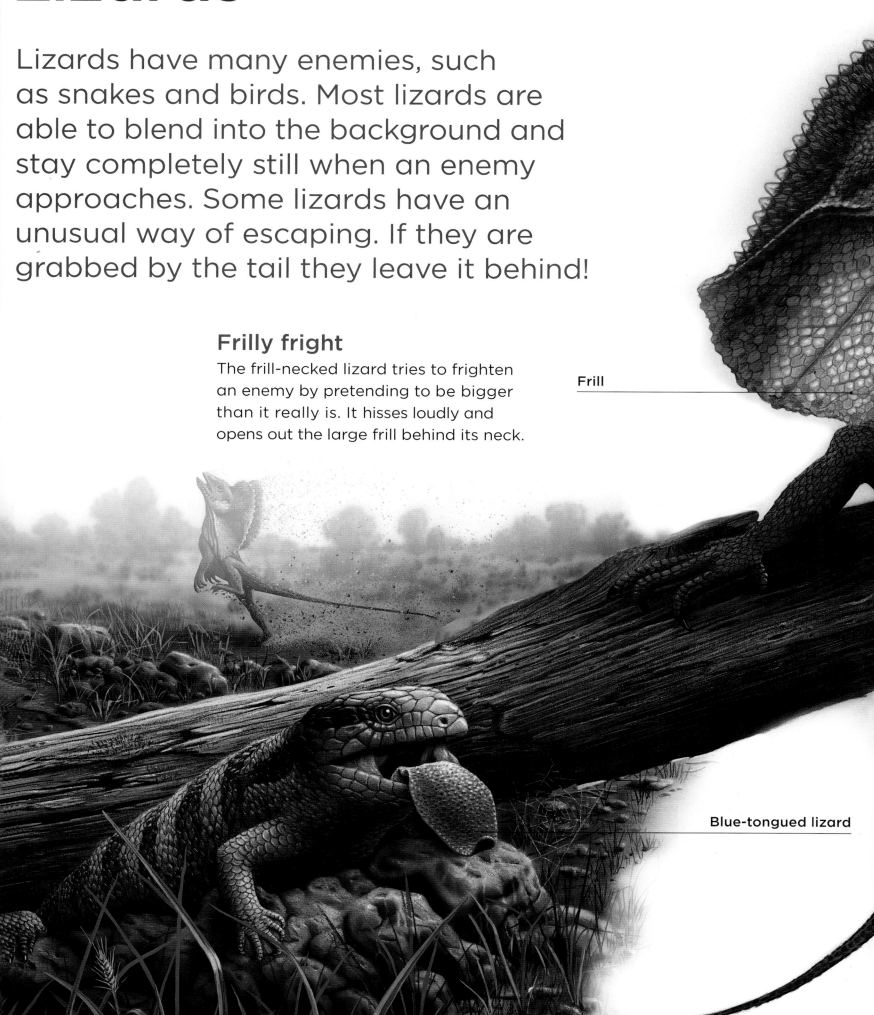

Frilly fright

The frill-necked lizard tries to frighten an enemy by pretending to be bigger than it really is. It hisses loudly and opens out the large frill behind its neck.

Frill

Blue-tongued lizard

Small lizards called geckos keep their eyes clean by licking them.

Monitor

Monitor lizards are tropical reptiles with strong bodies and long legs. They can run very fast and give a stinging lash with their tails.

Snakes

There are almost 2,400 kinds of snakes. They come in many different colors and sizes, but they all lay eggs and have scaly skin. Unlike you or me, snakes are cold-blooded. This means they have to lie in the sun, or in warm places, to stay at the correct temperature.

King cobras are the only snakes in the world that build nests for their young.

Different snakes have different patterns of scales on their skin.

Waiting for dinner

Carpet pythons are often colored black and yellow. Their patterned skin hides them as they lie in wait for passing prey.

Spitting cobra

This spitting cobra is spitting venom to defend itself. It can also open out a hood behind its head to make it look bigger than it actually is.

Hood

Scaly skin

Frogs

Frogs are amphibians. They spend part of their lives in water and part on land. Frogs lay their eggs in water. The eggs hatch into tadpoles, which lose their tails as they grow. Frogs eat insects, which they catch with their long, sticky tongues.

Frogs can live to between 2 and 40 years old.

Long leg

POISON SKIN

Poison-dart frogs get the poison that covers their skin from the insects they eat. If they are fed other foods, they become harmless.

Poisonous skin

Jump!
Frogs are good jumpers because they have long, powerful back legs, short bodies, and no tail to get in the way.

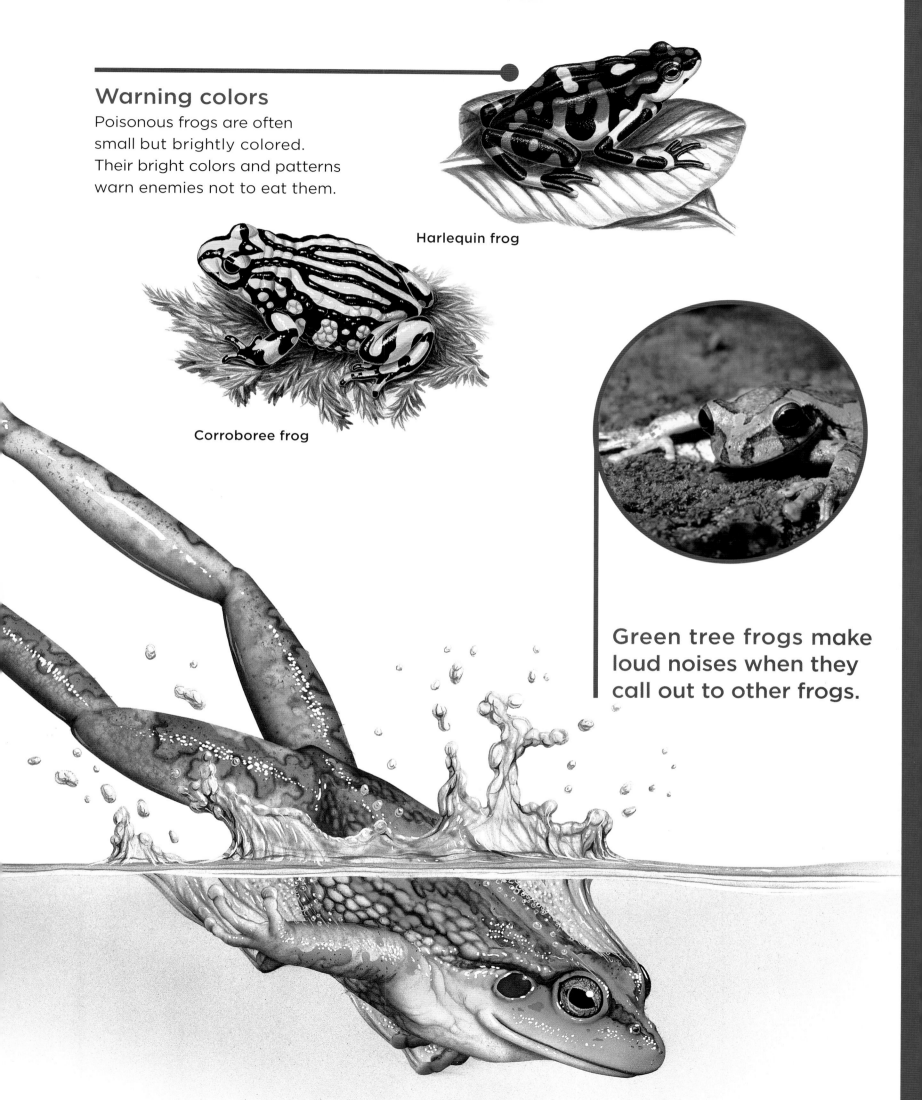

Warning colors

Poisonous frogs are often small but brightly colored. Their bright colors and patterns warn enemies not to eat them.

Harlequin frog

Corroboree frog

Green tree frogs make loud noises when they call out to other frogs.

Part-timers

There are animals that live on the land or fly in the air that never move far from the seas and oceans. This is because the sea is where they find their food. Many kinds of birds eat only fish. Polar bears often grab seals from the freezing polar waters.

Hungry bear

Polar bears are fierce hunters, especially when food is hard to find. This one has broken through ice to catch a baby beluga whale.

Hot and cold

Marine iguanas are the only lizards that live in the sea. They bask on rocks in the sun to warm up.

Marine iguanas sneeze out the salt they get from seawater.

Baby beluga whale

FLYING WITH FISH

Ospreys are birds that eat only fish. They catch the fish in their strong claws and carry them away to eat them.

Fantastic journeys

Some sea creatures make long journeys every year. We call these journeys "migrations." Some whales travel from warm parts of the world to cold polar waters. Here they eat the huge amounts of krill that they need to survive for the rest of the year.

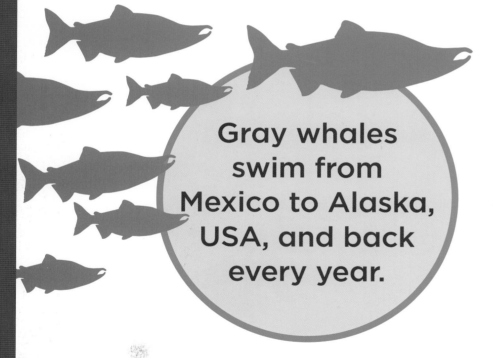

Gray whales swim from Mexico to Alaska, USA, and back every year.

Around the world

Arctic terns fly from the North Pole to the South Pole. Some of them fly around Antarctica before they make the return journey.

LONG-DISTANCE SWIMMERS

Sockeye salmon hatch into rivers. They then swim from here into the ocean. They return to the rivers to lay their eggs.

Female turtle

Baby turtle

Traveling turtles

Sea turtles spend a long time building up stores of fat. They need these stores so they can travel across the oceans to areas where they lay their eggs.

What is a bug?

Over three-quarters of all living creatures on Earth are bugs. Some have long legs, others have thin bodies, and many have wings. All bugs have a hard outer shell to protect them, and legs with joints. They live all around the world.

Wasp

Dragonfly

Caterpillars

Fly

SHAKE A LEG

Scorpions, ticks, centipedes, and spiders are not insects, but they are still called bugs. Insects have six legs, but scorpions, ticks, and spiders have eight legs. Centipedes can have as many as 400 legs!

Spider

Tick

Scorpion

Centipede

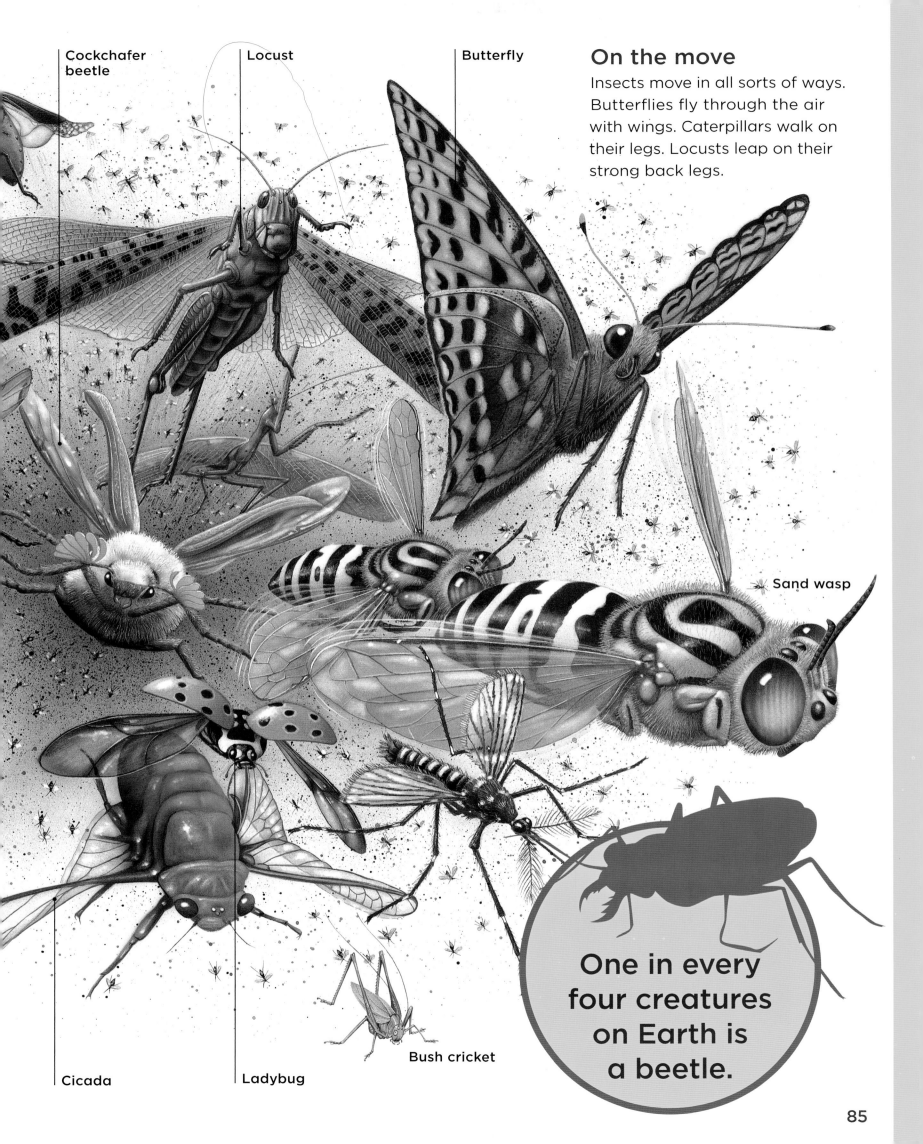

Cockchafer beetle

Locust

Butterfly

On the move

Insects move in all sorts of ways. Butterflies fly through the air with wings. Caterpillars walk on their legs. Locusts leap on their strong back legs.

Sand wasp

Cicada

Ladybug

Bush cricket

One in every four creatures on Earth is a beetle.

Bug action

Bugs are some of Earth's most common creatures: There are about 1.5 million kinds. Insects, spiders, scorpions, and ants are all called bugs. Bugs do not have backbones but have hard skeletons on the outside of their bodies.

This beautiful butterfly is feeding on nectar from inside flowers.

ATTACK

This spider, called a tarantula, is about to attack a lizard with its powerful fangs.

Tarantula

Lizard

Active and alert

Tiger beetles are fast runners and fliers. They can chase insects easily, and catch them with their strong jaws.

Ants can lift and carry more than 50 times their own weight.

Tiger beetle

Ant

Insects

There are more insects in the world than any other kind of animal. They all have six legs and a body made up of three parts. Insects have a hard shell on the outside that protects the body and forms an external skeleton.

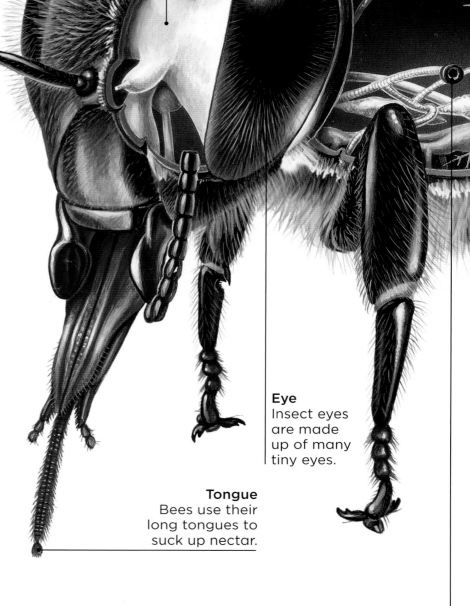

Brain

Antenna
Insects use antennae to feel, smell, and hear.

Eye
Insect eyes are made up of many tiny eyes.

Tongue
Bees use their long tongues to suck up nectar.

Most insects have claws on the end of each leg. These help them to cling to different surfaces.

Breathing holes
Insects breathe through holes on the sides of their body.

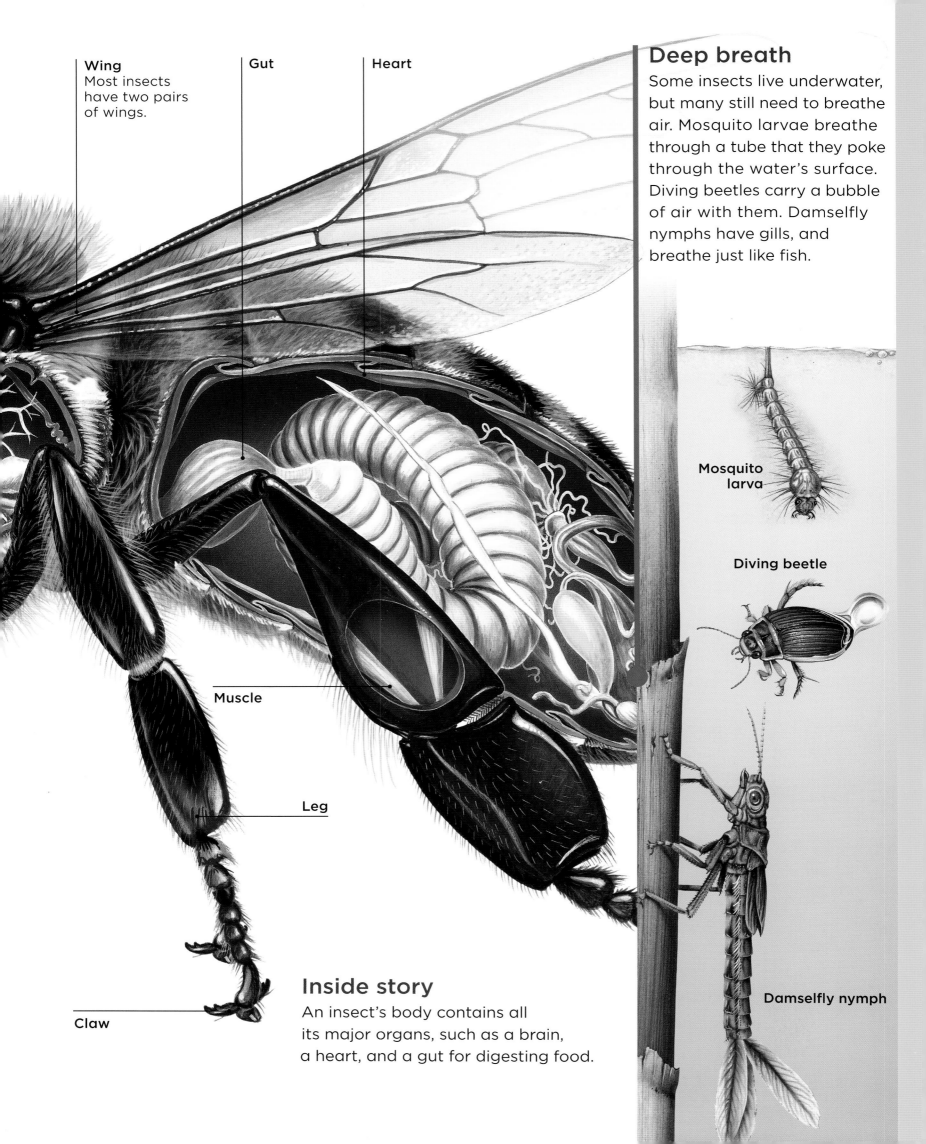

Wing
Most insects have two pairs of wings.

Gut

Heart

Muscle

Leg

Claw

Deep breath
Some insects live underwater, but many still need to breathe air. Mosquito larvae breathe through a tube that they poke through the water's surface. Diving beetles carry a bubble of air with them. Damselfly nymphs have gills, and breathe just like fish.

Mosquito larva

Diving beetle

Damselfly nymph

Inside story
An insect's body contains all its major organs, such as a brain, a heart, and a gut for digesting food.

Crickets and cockroaches

Crickets and grasshoppers have strong back legs, which they use to leap high into the air. Cockroaches cannot jump. They scuttle about quickly on their legs. They can go for months without food, and can survive in places where no other insect could live.

Field cricket

Green banana roach

German cockroach

Little roach

The tiny ant cockroach is the smallest in the world. It is only as long as a grain of rice.

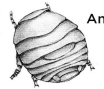

Ant cockroach

Madagascan hissing cockroach

A cockroach will eat cardboard if there is no other food around.

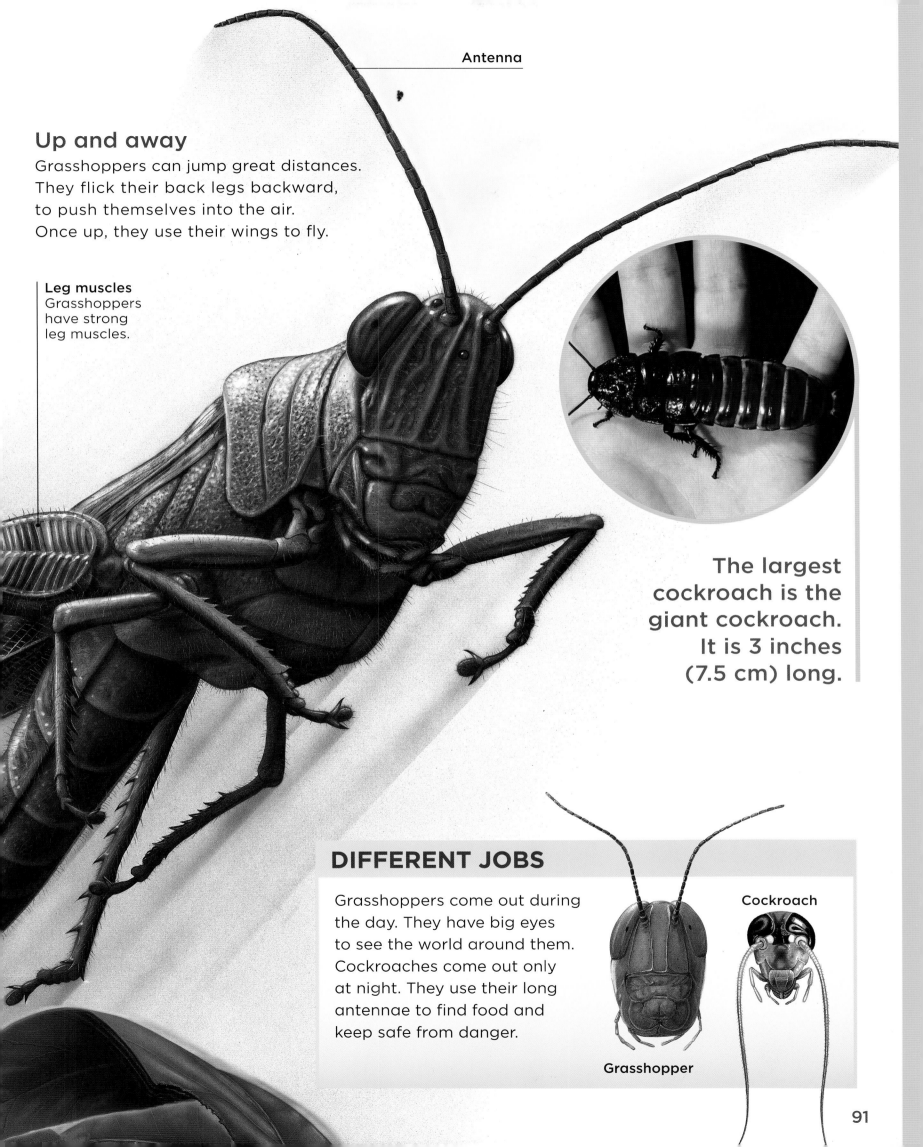

Antenna

Up and away

Grasshoppers can jump great distances.
They flick their back legs backward,
to push themselves into the air.
Once up, they use their wings to fly.

Leg muscles
Grasshoppers
have strong
leg muscles.

The largest
cockroach is the
giant cockroach.
It is 3 inches
(7.5 cm) long.

DIFFERENT JOBS

Grasshoppers come out during
the day. They have big eyes
to see the world around them.
Cockroaches come out only
at night. They use their long
antennae to find food and
keep safe from danger.

Cockroach

Grasshopper

True bugs

We call many small creatures "bugs," but bugs are actually a special group of insects. They all have long, thin mouths that they use like straws to suck up food. Some bugs use this special mouth to kill and eat other animals. Other bugs feed on plants.

Big mouth

The mouth of the assassin bug is long and sharp. It uses it to stab its victim. It then sucks up the juices inside.

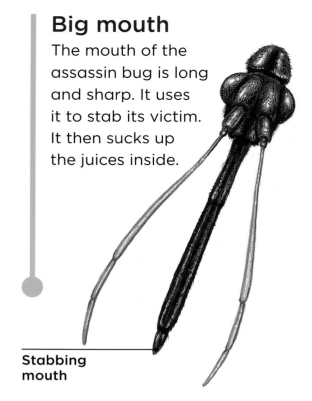

Stabbing mouth

Water scorpion

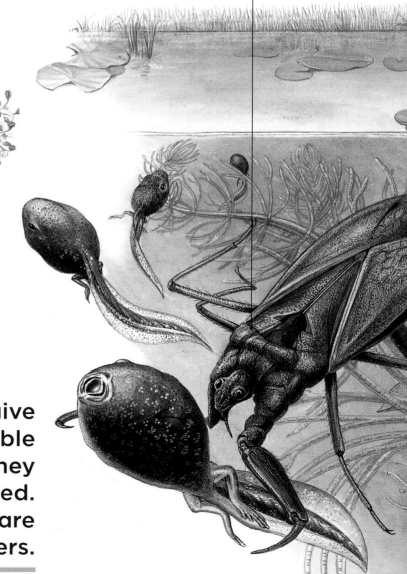

Flower food

This jester bug sucks up nectar from flowers with its long mouth.

Stink bugs give off a terrible smell when they are threatened. This is to scare away attackers.

Underwater

Ponds are home to many different kinds of bugs. Some live under the water, and others live on the surface. All hunt for food with their long needle-like mouths.

Giant water bugs are so huge they can catch fish.

Water strider

Water boatman

Beetles

There are more than 400,000 kinds of beetles in the world. Beetles have strong front wings, which they use to cover their delicate back wings. This hard covering also keeps them safe from other animals that would like to eat them.

Big fight

Male Hercules beetles use their large horns to fight each other for a female beetle. For their size, Hercules beetles are the strongest creatures on Earth.

Female beetle

Fireflies are actually beetles, not flies.

Ladybugs

Ladybugs are brightly colored to warn other animals that they taste bad.

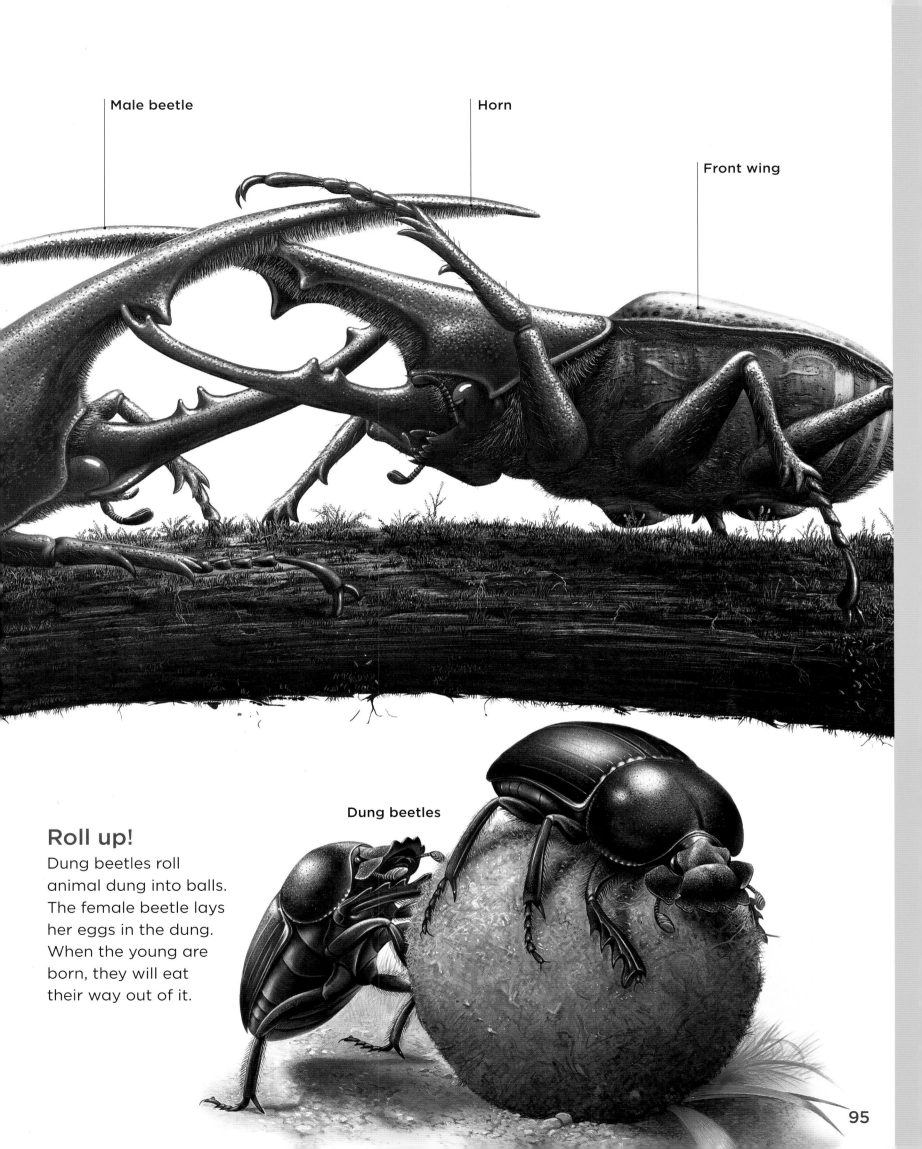

Male beetle

Horn

Front wing

Dung beetles

Roll up!

Dung beetles roll animal dung into balls. The female beetle lays her eggs in the dung. When the young are born, they will eat their way out of it.

Flies and dragonflies

Flies and dragonflies are both good at flying. Flies use one pair of wings to fly. Some flies eat insects, while others feed on rotting meat and plants. Dragonflies have two pairs of wings. They eat insects, such as mosquitoes.

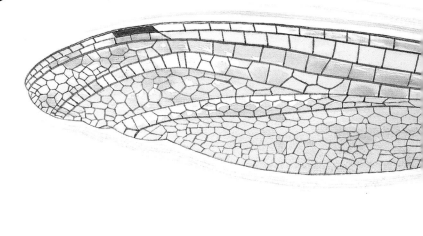

Young flies are called maggots. They are blind and have no legs.

Hairy bee fly
This fly sticks its long, thin mouth into flowers to get the nectar inside.

House flies have sticky feet. This is why they can walk on the ceiling.

FOOD FOR FLIES

All flies eat liquid food. They can make a meal out of almost anything.

House flies
These flies pour their acid saliva onto food to turn it into liquid, before slurping it up.

Fruit flies
These flies eat the juices from rotting fruit.

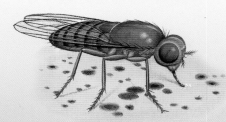

Mosquitoes
These small flies feed on blood.

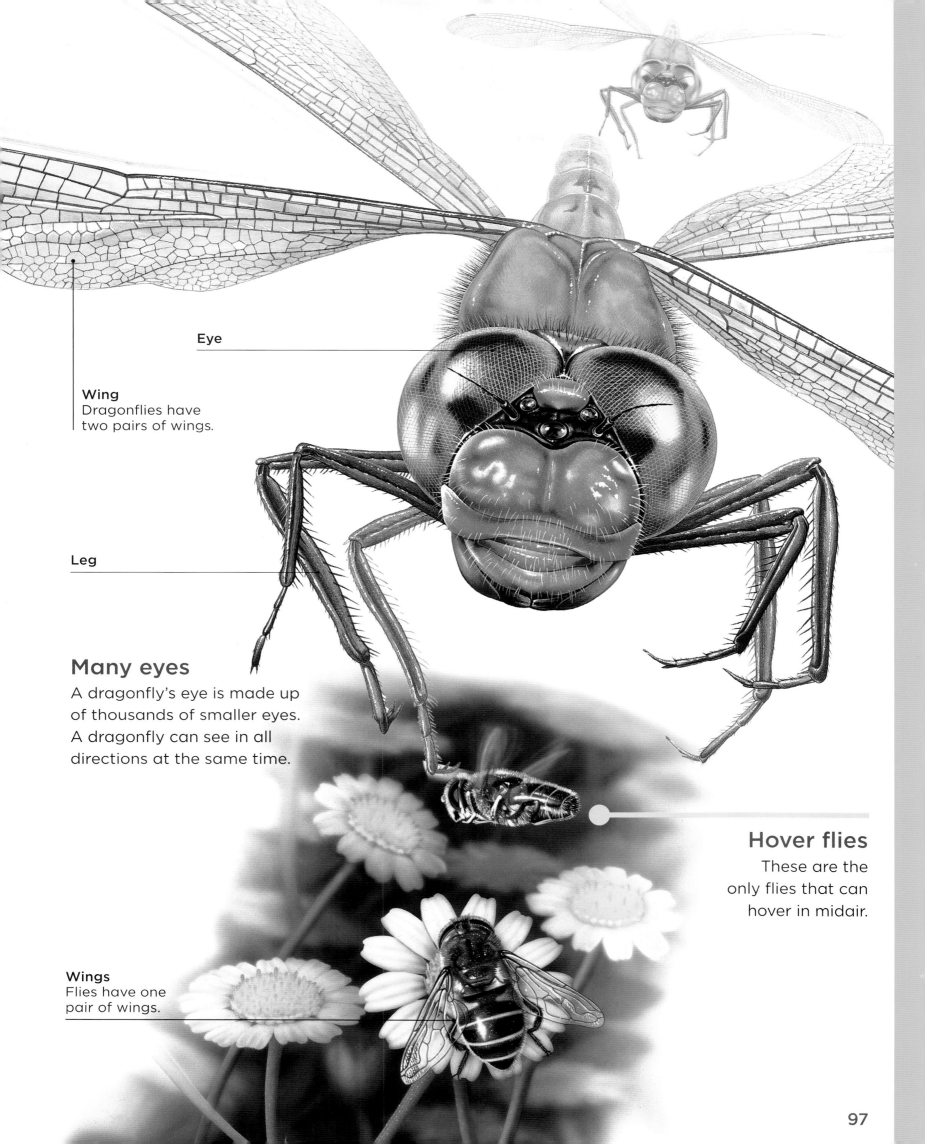

Eye

Wing
Dragonflies have
two pairs of wings.

Leg

Many eyes

A dragonfly's eye is made up
of thousands of smaller eyes.
A dragonfly can see in all
directions at the same time.

Hover flies

These are the
only flies that can
hover in midair.

Wings
Flies have one
pair of wings.

Butterflies and moths

Butterflies and moths have two pairs of wings, and a pair of long, thin antennae sprouting from their heads. They use their antennae to find food and a partner. Butterflies come out only during the day. Moths usually come out at night.

Colorful creatures
Butterflies and moths come in many colors and patterns. Their colors often match the flowers they live on.

Yellow emperor moth

Madagascan sunset moth

Orange-barred sulfur butterfly

SPOT THE DIFFERENCE

You can tell the difference between a moth and a butterfly by looking at their wings and antennae. Butterflies hold their wings together when they rest. Moths hold them flat. Butterflies have club-shaped antennae. Moths have feathery or plain antennae.

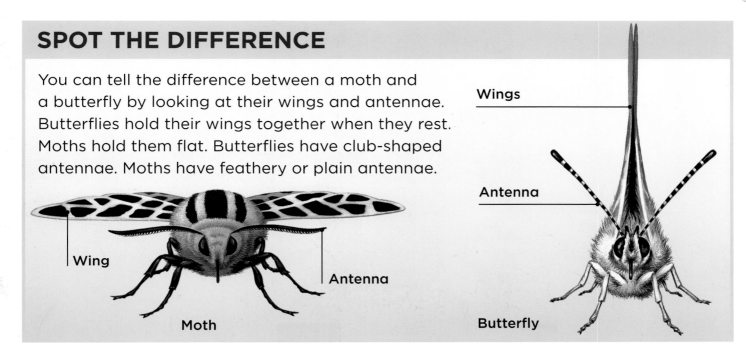

Wings

Antenna

Wing

Antenna

Moth

Butterfly

Swallowtail butterfly

Cabbage
white butterfly

Dinnertime

Butterflies and moths
feed on nectar from
flowers. They use their
curly tongue to eat.

Eighty-eight
butterfly

Bees and wasps

Bees and wasps are different from most other insects because they all have thin waists. Most types of bees and wasps live in groups. Together, they build nests, where they raise their young and store food.

Swarming bees

Bee houses

Bees live in nests called hives. The hives are made of wax. The bees use the hives to store honey and look after their young.

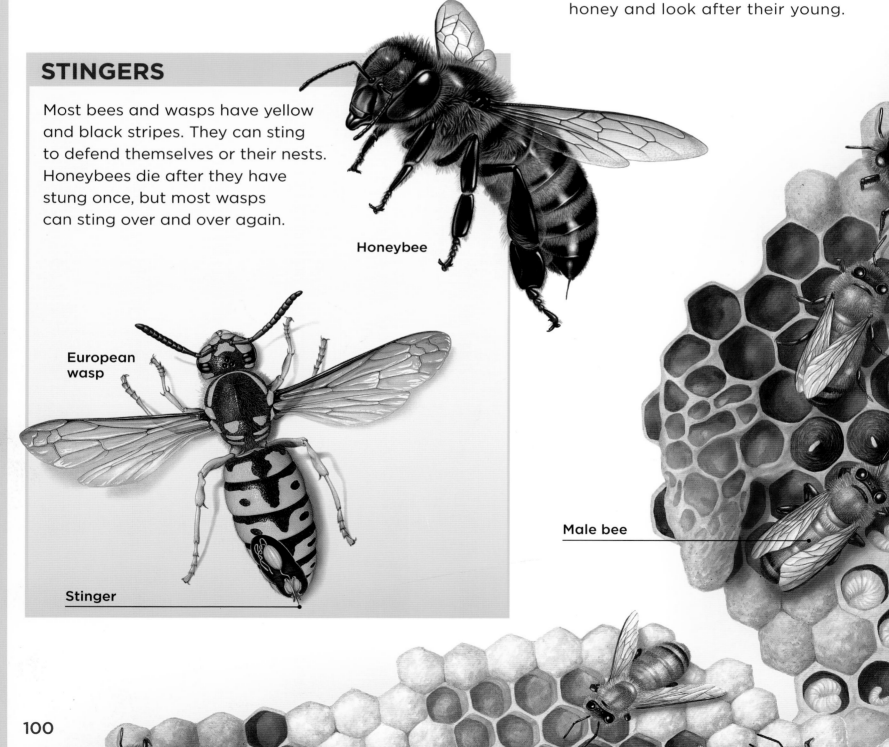

STINGERS

Most bees and wasps have yellow and black stripes. They can sting to defend themselves or their nests. Honeybees die after they have stung once, but most wasps can sting over and over again.

Honeybee

European wasp

Stinger

Male bee

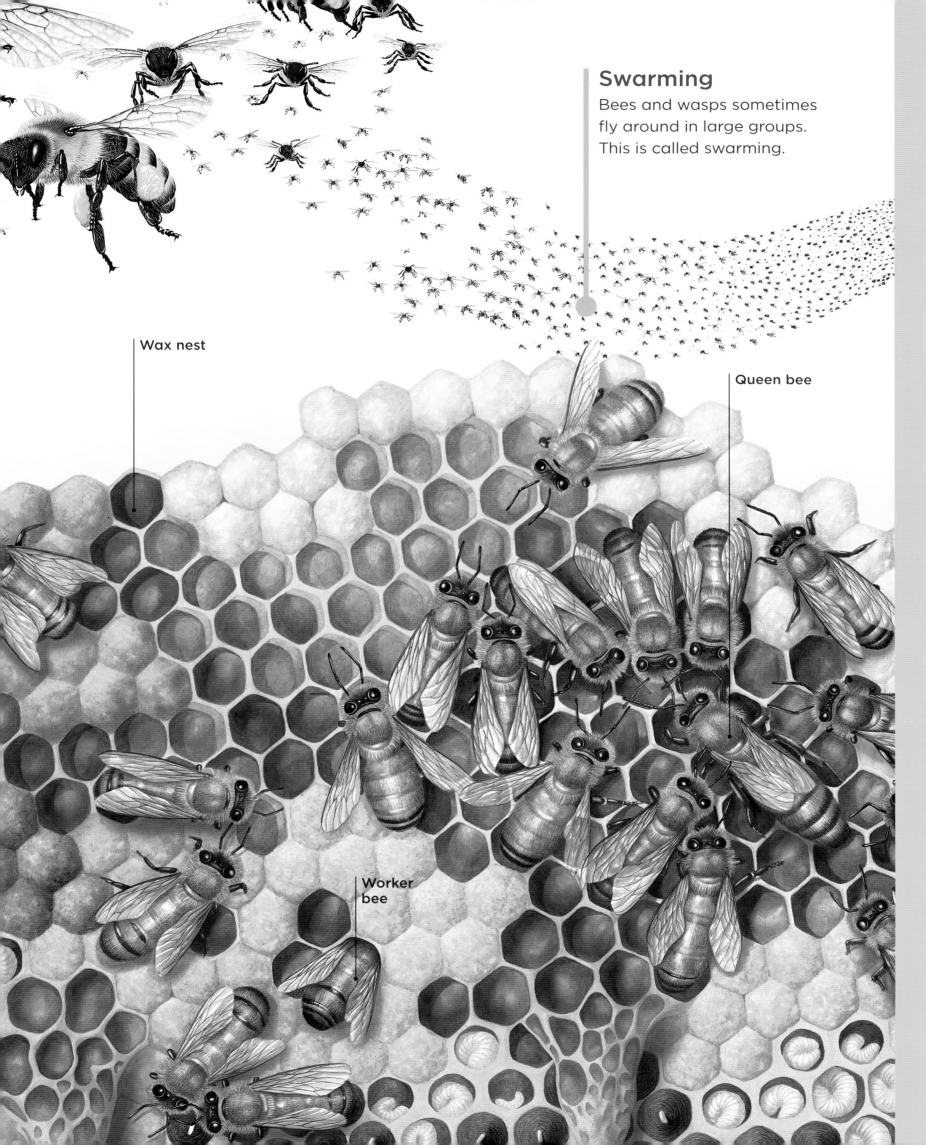

Swarming

Bees and wasps sometimes fly around in large groups. This is called swarming.

Wax nest

Queen bee

Worker bee

Ants

Most ants live and travel in large groups. They build nests that can be underground, in plants, or even up trees. Ant groups are made up of at least two types of ant—the worker ants and the queen ant. The single queen ant produces all the baby ants for the group.

Termites are close relatives of ants. They build very tall nests.

MEETING

When two ants meet, they use their antennae to smell each other. That way, they can find out if they are from the same family.

Cutting leaves

Leaf-cutter ants feed on a special type of fungus that grows on leaves. Worker ants chop the leaves into small pieces. They then carry them back to the nest to be prepared for eating.

Same family, different jobs

Queen ant
She lays all eggs
for the nest.

Soldier ants
They protect the nest.

Male ants
They mate with
the queen ant.

Worker ants
They collect food.

Ants can live in groups as large as 300 million!

Flying high

Flying is a great way for an insect to get about. It helps it find a new place to live, food to eat, and a new mate to start a family. Flying also helps it to get away from danger quickly. Most insects fly by themselves. Others fly in large groups called swarms.

KINDS OF WINGS

Every kind of insect has a unique set of wings.

Fly

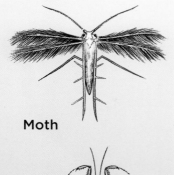
Moth

Mantis

A dragonfly can move as fast as an express train.

Head spin

This flea beetle does not fly, but it jumps far through the air. It spins over and over as it goes.

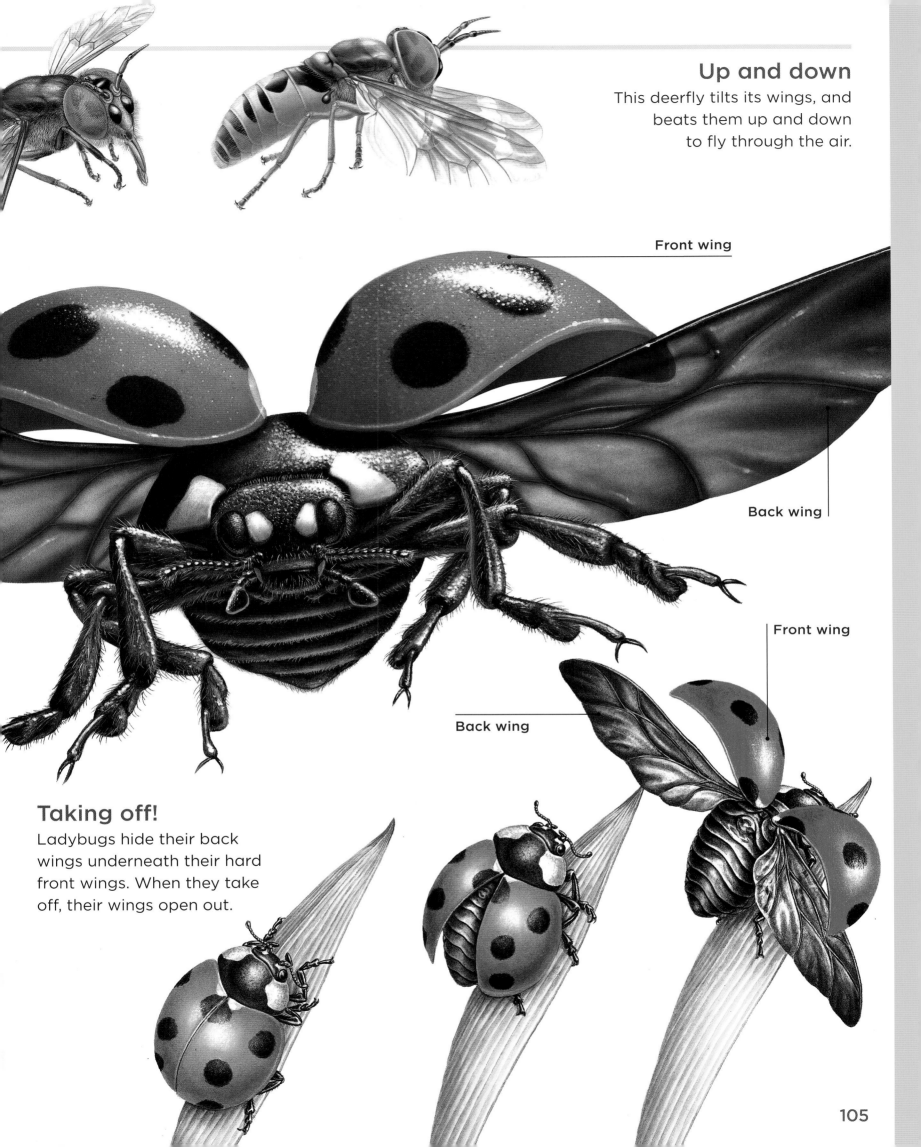

This deerfly tilts its wings, and beats them up and down to fly through the air.

Front wing

Back wing

Front wing

Back wing

Taking off!

Ladybugs hide their back wings underneath their hard front wings. When they take off, their wings open out.

105

Insect world

It is important for insects to know what is going on around them. Just like us, they do this by sight, smell, touch, taste, and sound. Some insects have developed senses that are much stronger than those of humans.

Super sight
This horsefly's eyes are made up of thousands of smaller eyes, called eyelets.

What a human sees

What a bee sees

Special sight
Bees see differently from humans. This helps them to see which flowers will have pollen to eat.

Weird ears
Grasshoppers call to each other by rubbing their back legs against their wings. They hear these calls through special "ears" on their abdomens.

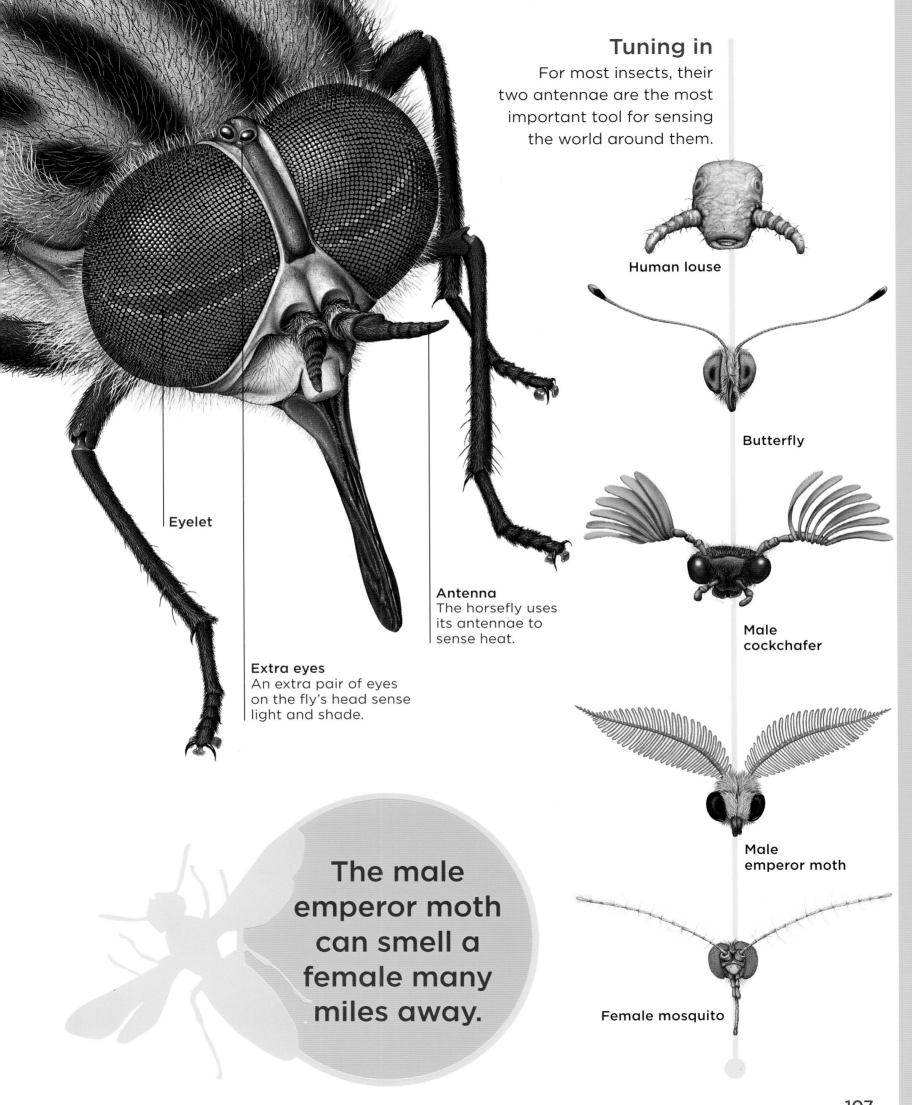

Eyelet

Extra eyes
An extra pair of eyes on the fly's head sense light and shade.

Antenna
The horsefly uses its antennae to sense heat.

Tuning in

For most insects, their two antennae are the most important tool for sensing the world around them.

Human louse

Butterfly

Male cockchafer

Male emperor moth

Female mosquito

The male emperor moth can smell a female many miles away.

Finding food

Insects spend most of their lives finding and eating food. Some insects eat plants. Some insects eat other animals. Others eat a bit of both. A few insects even survive by drinking blood!

The **red coloring** used in some foods is made from **crushed beetles.**

Meat eater
This praying mantis uses its fast front legs to catch insects to eat.

Praying mantis

Butterfly

Hickory horned
devil caterpillar

Plant eater

This caterpillar has strong
jaws to chew through its
favorite food of tough leaves.

Changing forms

Some insect babies are called nymphs. Nymphs look like small adults, without the wings. Other insect babies are called larvae. Larvae look very different from their parents. Both nymphs and larvae grow out of their young bodies and change into adults.

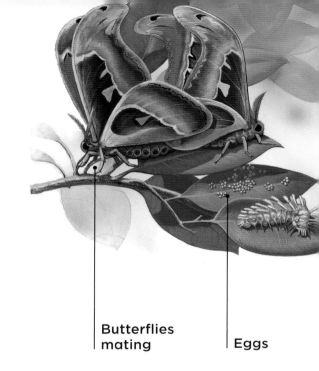

Butterflies mating

Eggs

Growing larger

A baby cicada is called a nymph. As the nymph gets older, it sheds its outer shell to make room for its growing body.

INSIDER

A bee starts life as a larva. It grows inside its waxy cell. While it grows, other bees bring it food to eat. Soon it will turn into an adult bee.

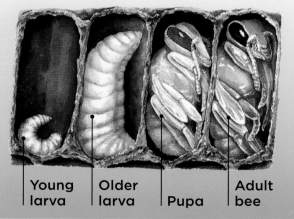

Young larva | Older larva | Pupa | Adult bee

Water baby

Dragonflies start life underwater. A dragonfly nymph can live underwater for five years. As it grows larger, it sheds its skin. When it is fully grown, it crawls out of the water and flies away.

Dragonfly laying eggs

Eggs

All change

A butterfly starts life as an egg, which grows into a larva. Butterfly larvae are called caterpillars. After a few weeks, the caterpillar's skin changes and it turns into a pupa. The adult butterfly forms inside the pupa. Once it is ready, the butterfly breaks out of its case and flies away.

Caterpillar

Pupa

Adult butterfly

Dragonflies mating

Nymph

Crawling out of its shell

Adult dragonfly

Spiders

There are more than 35,000 kinds of spiders. They are different from insects because they move on eight legs instead of six. They also have bodies that are divided into two parts. Lots of people are afraid of them, but most spiders are harmless to you and me.

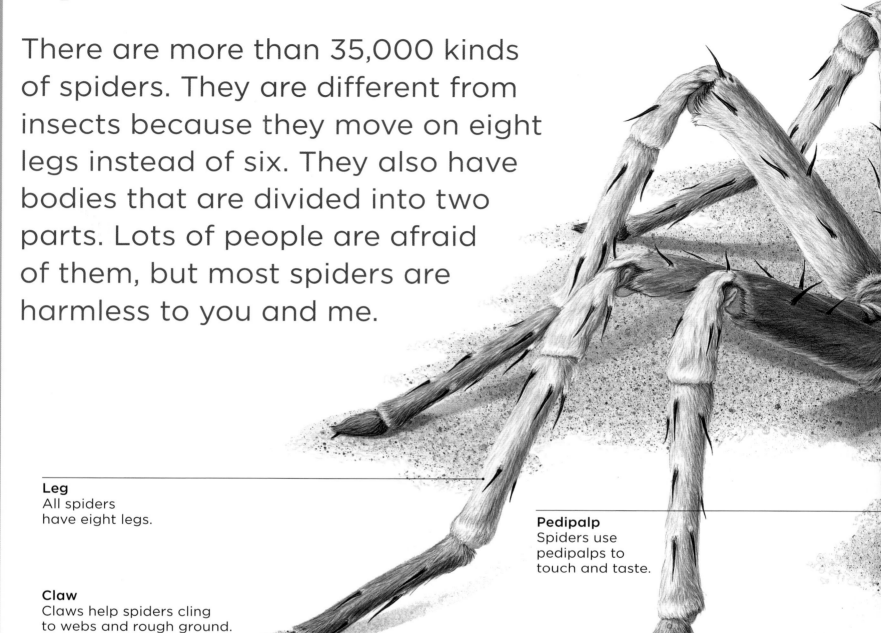

Leg
All spiders have eight legs.

Claw
Claws help spiders cling to webs and rough ground.

Pedipalp
Spiders use pedipalps to touch and taste.

SPIDER EYES

You can tell a lot about a spider by its eyes.

Ogre-faced spider
This spider has huge eyes that it uses to hunt in the dark.

Crab spider
The crab spider has good eyes for seeing prey that is close by.

Huntsman spider
This spider has spread-out eyes that are good for hunting.

Woodlouse-eating spider
This spider has to use its sense of touch to find prey because its eyes are very small.

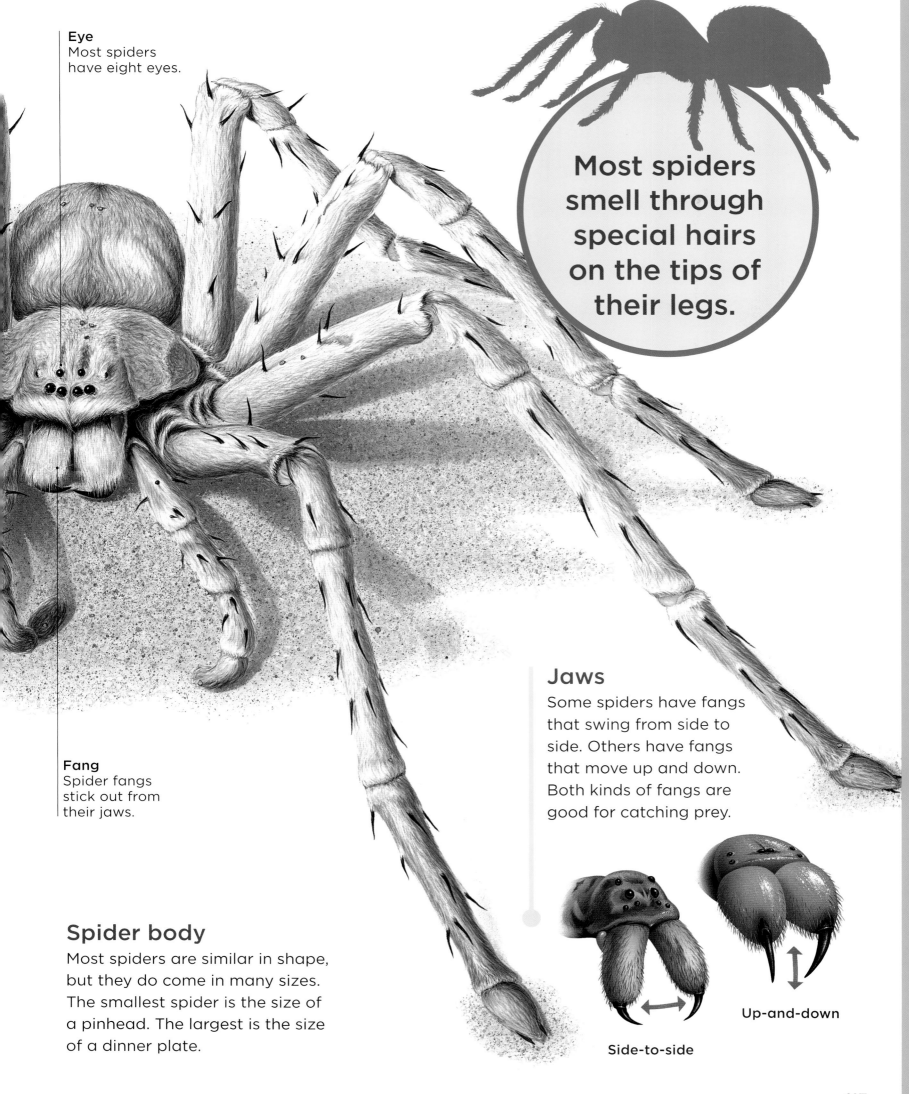

Eye
Most spiders have eight eyes.

Most spiders smell through special hairs on the tips of their legs.

Fang
Spider fangs stick out from their jaws.

Jaws
Some spiders have fangs that swing from side to side. Others have fangs that move up and down. Both kinds of fangs are good for catching prey.

Spider body
Most spiders are similar in shape, but they do come in many sizes. The smallest spider is the size of a pinhead. The largest is the size of a dinner plate.

Side-to-side

Up-and-down

Web spinners

Some spiders catch their food in a web. Most strands of the web are strong and sticky. Unlucky insects that fly into the web get stuck in these strands and cannot escape. The spider wraps them in more strands until it is ready to eat.

Silk strands

Spiders make their webs from silk. They know when something has landed on the web because they can feel the strands move.

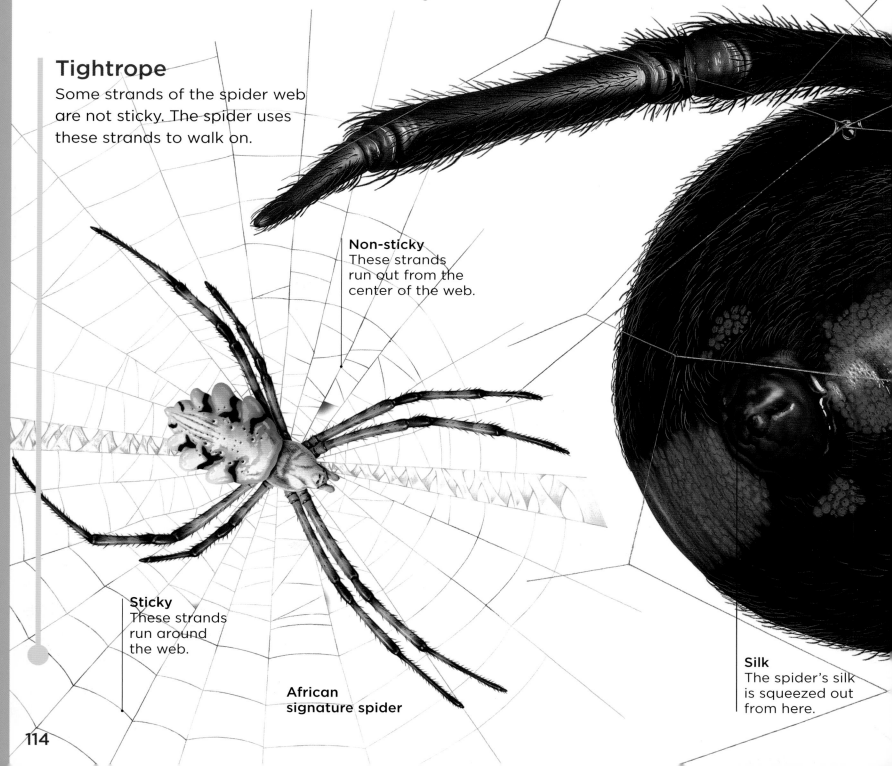

Tightrope
Some strands of the spider web are not sticky. The spider uses these strands to walk on.

Non-sticky
These strands run out from the center of the web.

Sticky
These strands run around the web.

African signature spider

Silk
The spider's silk is squeezed out from here.

Redback spider

The strands of a
spider's web are easy
to see when covered
in morning dew.

FANCY FEET

Spiders that build webs have three
claws on each foot. The claws hook
on to the strands of the web.

Claw

Hunting spiders

Spiders that do not build webs to catch their food are called hunting spiders. Some jump or run quickly to catch their victims. Others hide and wait for their meals to come to them.

Jumping spiders have large eyes. They can see their prey from far away.

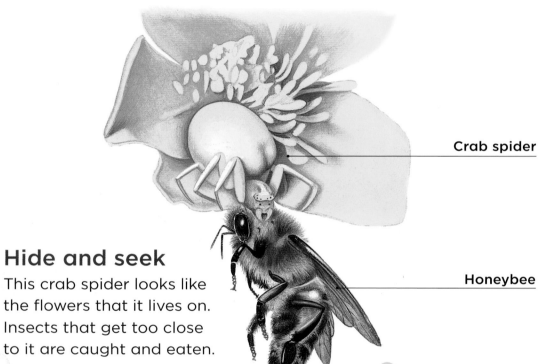

Crab spider

Honeybee

Hide and seek

This crab spider looks like the flowers that it lives on. Insects that get too close to it are caught and eaten.

CLEVER SILK

These spiders do not build webs, but they do use silk to hunt.

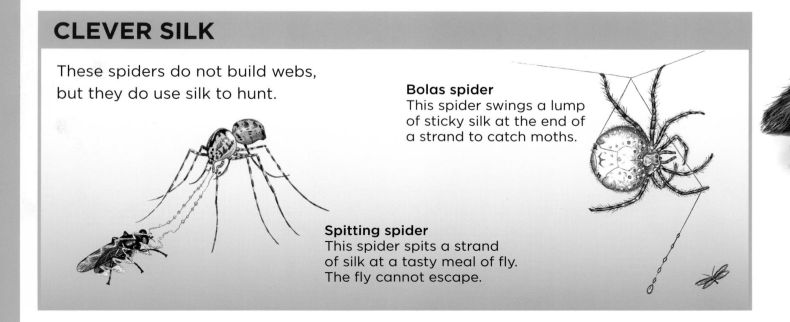

Bolas spider
This spider swings a lump of sticky silk at the end of a strand to catch moths.

Spitting spider
This spider spits a strand of silk at a tasty meal of fly. The fly cannot escape.

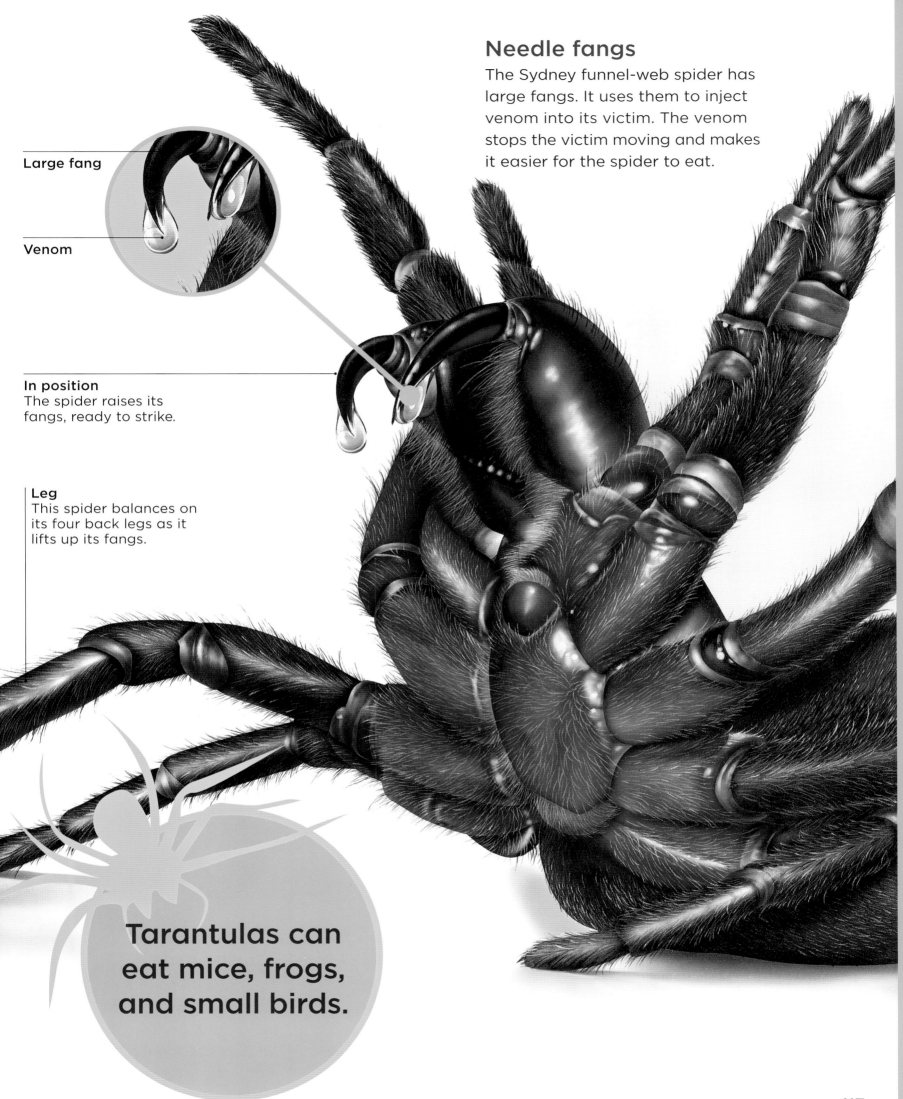

Large fang

Venom

In position
The spider raises its fangs, ready to strike.

Leg
This spider balances on its four back legs as it lifts up its fangs.

Needle fangs
The Sydney funnel-web spider has large fangs. It uses them to inject venom into its victim. The venom stops the victim moving and makes it easier for the spider to eat.

Tarantulas can eat mice, frogs, and small birds.

Spider survival

Tarantula

Many animals, including birds, frogs, and some insects, like to make a meal of spiders. Luckily, spiders have lots of ways to avoid being eaten. If hiding or running away does not work, then they may have to fight back.

Big and hairy

Some tarantulas flick their body hairs at their attackers. The hairs stick in the skin and are itchy and painful. Other tarantulas make a hissing sound to scare enemies away.

ROLL UP

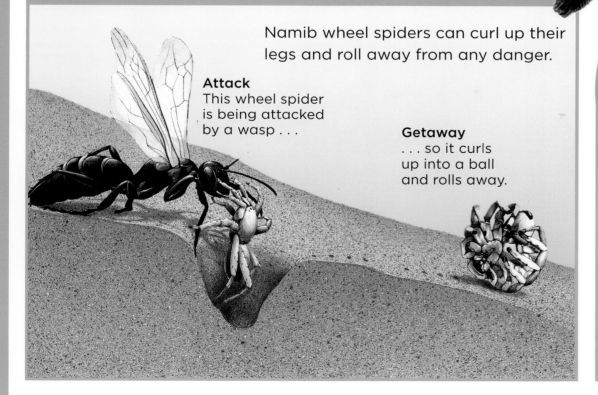

Namib wheel spiders can curl up their legs and roll away from any danger.

Attack
This wheel spider is being attacked by a wasp . . .

Getaway
. . . so it curls up into a ball and rolls away.

Spider hair

The hairs on a spider are sensitive to movement in the air and on the ground. Spiders use them to feel if an enemy is coming near.

Wasp

Trapdoor spider

Bottoms up

This trapdoor spider blocks its burrow with its own backside to avoid being stung by a wasp. The wasp's stinger cannot break through the thick skin.

Some spiders will shed a leg to escape from an attacker.

119

Showing off

Spiders use smell, sight, touch, hearing, and taste to defend themselves, catch food, and find out what is happening in the world around them. Spiders also use senses to understand other spiders and to find mates.

Body talk

Jumping spiders do a special dance when they are getting to know each other. The male waves his legs in the air to attract the female and to show off his bright colors.

Female spider

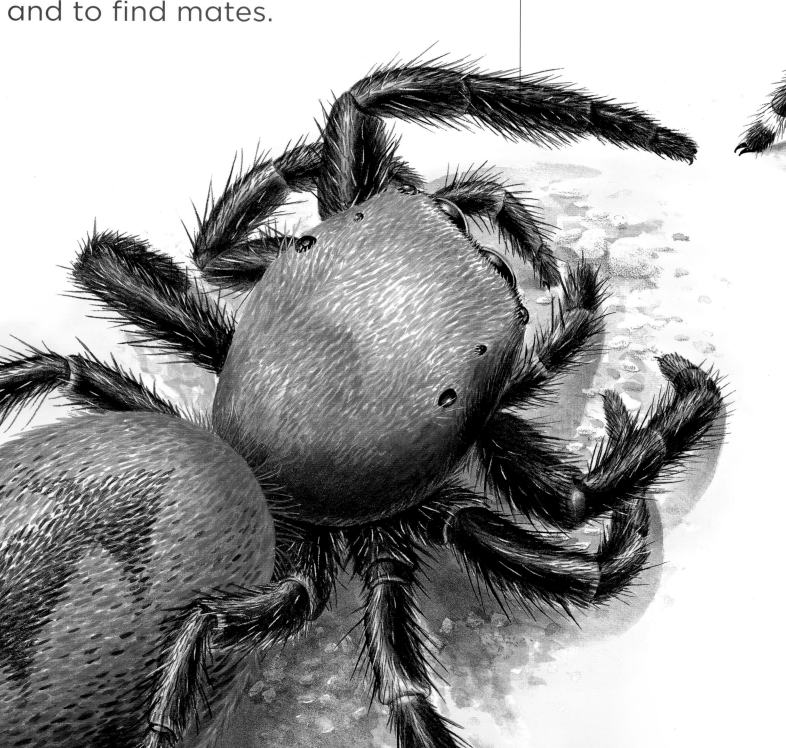

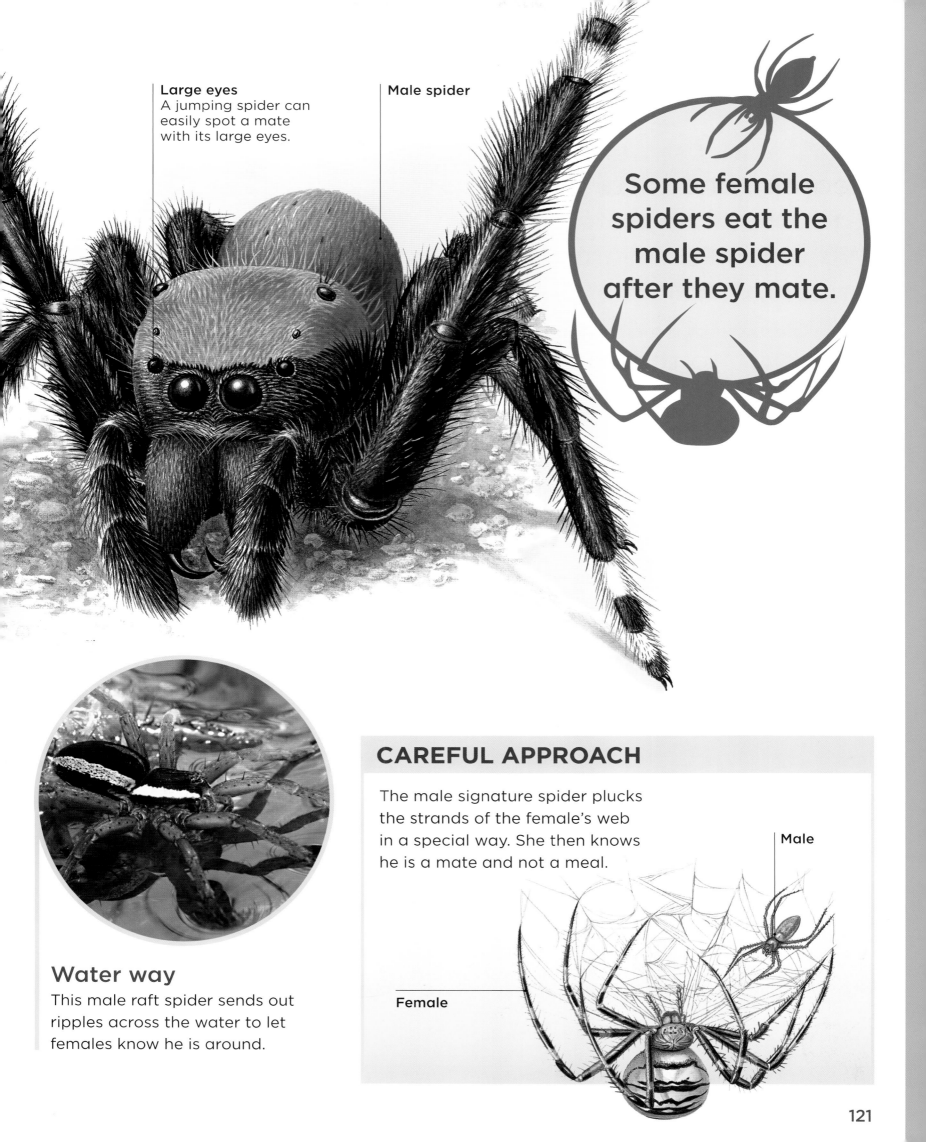

Large eyes
A jumping spider can easily spot a mate with its large eyes.

Male spider

Some female spiders eat the male spider after they mate.

Water way
This male raft spider sends out ripples across the water to let females know he is around.

CAREFUL APPROACH

The male signature spider plucks the strands of the female's web in a special way. She then knows he is a mate and not a meal.

Male

Female

Spider life

Every spider starts life as an egg. Most mother spiders wrap their eggs in silk to protect them. When they are born, baby spiders look like tiny versions of their parents. Most spiders give birth to thousands of babies, but only a few live to become adults.

ALL CHANGE

Spiders have to shed their skin as they grow. They usually stop shedding their skin when they become adults.

Head first
The spider breaks out of its old skin, head first.

Legs next
It eases out its slender legs.

Out
Once it is out, it leaves the old skin behind.

Good mother
The nursery-web spider uses silk to make a safe nest for her babies to live in. She also stays close to protect them.

Mother spider

Baby carrier
Wolf spider babies cling to their mother's body after being born.

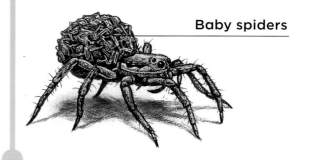

Baby spiders

Time to fly

Some baby spiders leave their nest by
flying through the air on tiny threads of silk.
This is called ballooning. The wind carries
them to a new place to live.

Baby spider

Spider relatives

Scorpions, mites, and ticks are close relatives of spiders. Like spiders, they all have eight legs. Scorpions can deliver a nasty sting, but most are harmless to humans. Ticks and mites are small and often live on other animals.

Some scorpions are so large that they can eat frogs.

Night glow

All scorpions glow in the dark under special types of light. No one is sure why.

POWERFUL JAWS

This wind scorpion has very powerful jaws, which it uses to catch prey.

Getting close

Scorpions use their tails to kill their prey and to fight off enemies. These scorpions are dancing together before mating. They grab each other's pincers and hold their tails high in the air.

Ticks and mites

Ticks drink blood. Most mites are so small you can see them only with a microscope.

Tick

Velvet mite

Stinger
Poison comes out of the stinger on the end of the scorpion's tail.

What is a dinosaur?

Dinosaurs were very special reptiles that lived on Earth for about 160 million years. Some dinosaurs were as small as chickens but others were huge. They had scaly skin and their eggs had shells. Dinosaurs walked upright and stood on either four legs or two.

Brachiosaurus

Deinonychus

Hypsilophodon

Ouranosaurus

Tyrannosaurus

Dinosaur parade

There were at least 1,000 different types of dinosaurs. There were dinosaurs with horns and crests and others with spikes and razor-sharp claws.

Parasaurolophus

Struthiomimus

Triceratops

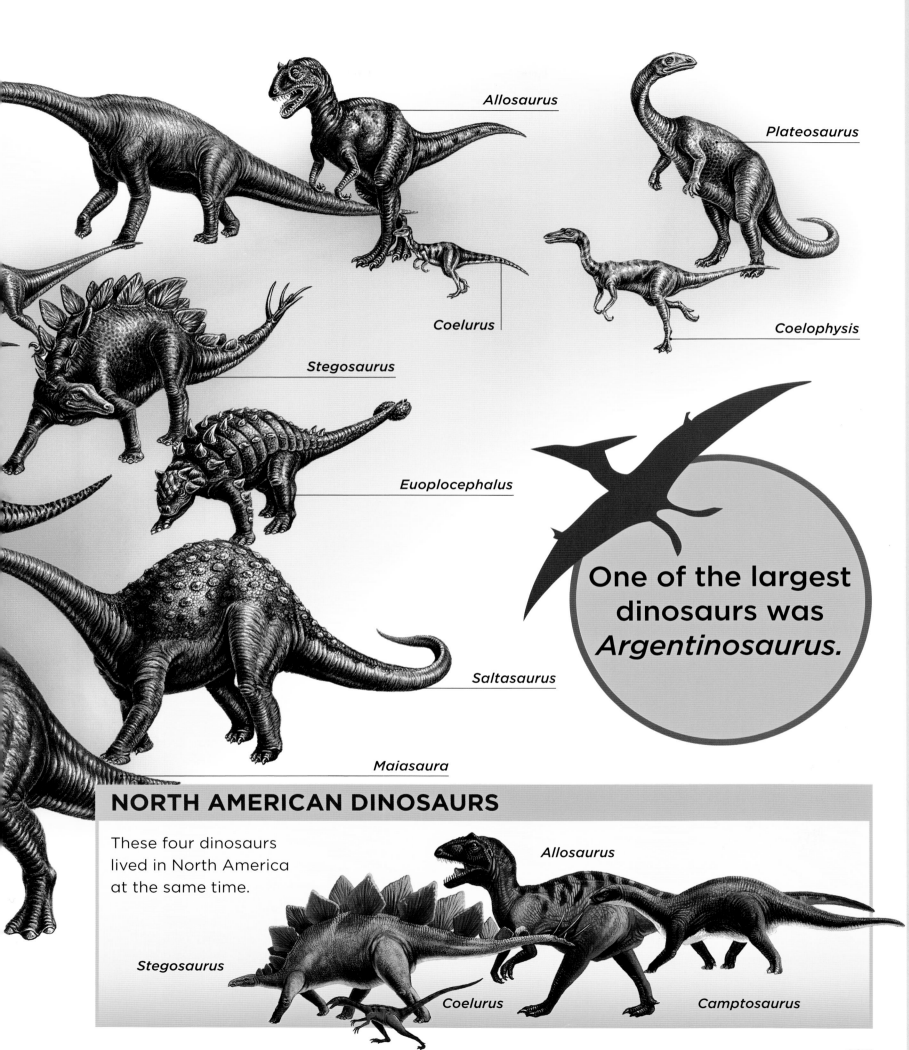

Allosaurus

Plateosaurus

Coelurus

Coelophysis

Stegosaurus

Euoplocephalus

One of the largest dinosaurs was *Argentinosaurus.*

Saltasaurus

Maiasaura

NORTH AMERICAN DINOSAURS

These four dinosaurs lived in North America at the same time.

Allosaurus

Stegosaurus

Coelurus

Camptosaurus

Age of dinosaurs

Dinosaurs first appeared on Earth about 228 million years ago. Millions of years later, as Earth's landmasses drifted apart, the weather changed. The cooler, wet weather was perfect for dinosaurs, so many more developed. About 65 million years ago, these extraordinary creatures disappeared.

Catching food
Dilophosaurus could run after its prey on its strong back legs.

Tyrannosaurus

Pteranodon

Dinosaur times

The time that dinosaurs roamed Earth is divided into three periods—the Triassic, Jurassic, and Cretaceous. The dinosaurs on these pages come from the three different periods.

Diplodocus

Dinosaurs lived millions of years before our first human ancestors.

Inside a dinosaur

All dinosaurs had skeletons inside their bodies. These gave them strength and protected their soft organs. Dinosaurs also had large muscles that helped them move around. The skeletons, muscles, and organs were all covered with a layer of thick, scaly skin.

Long journey

Apatosaurus ate a huge amount of leaves. The leaves traveled from its mouth to its stomach, along a long tube.

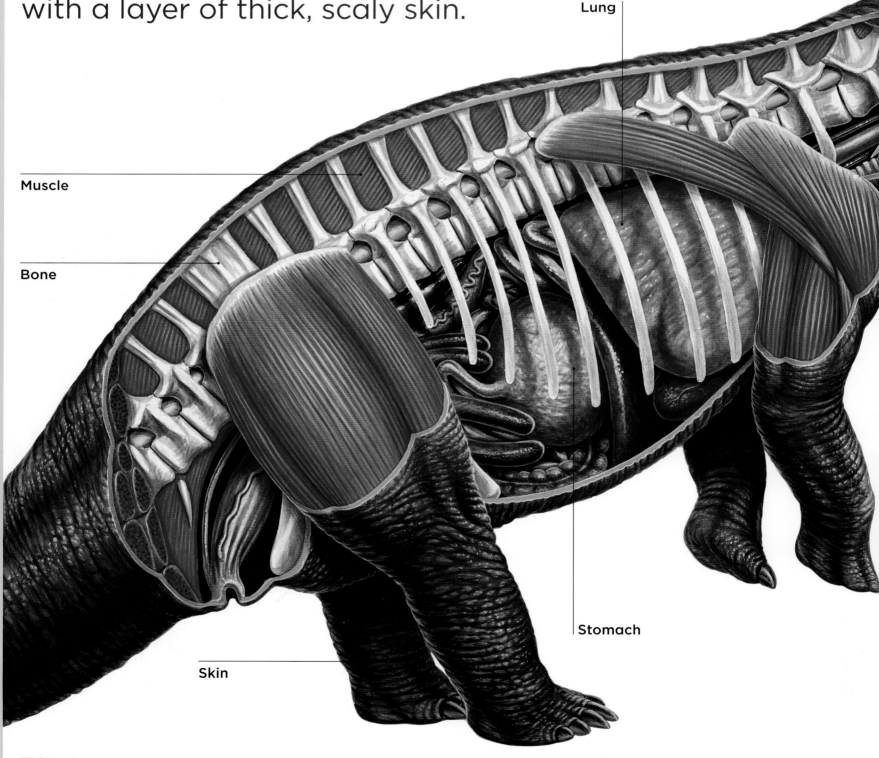

Lung

Muscle

Bone

Stomach

Skin

130

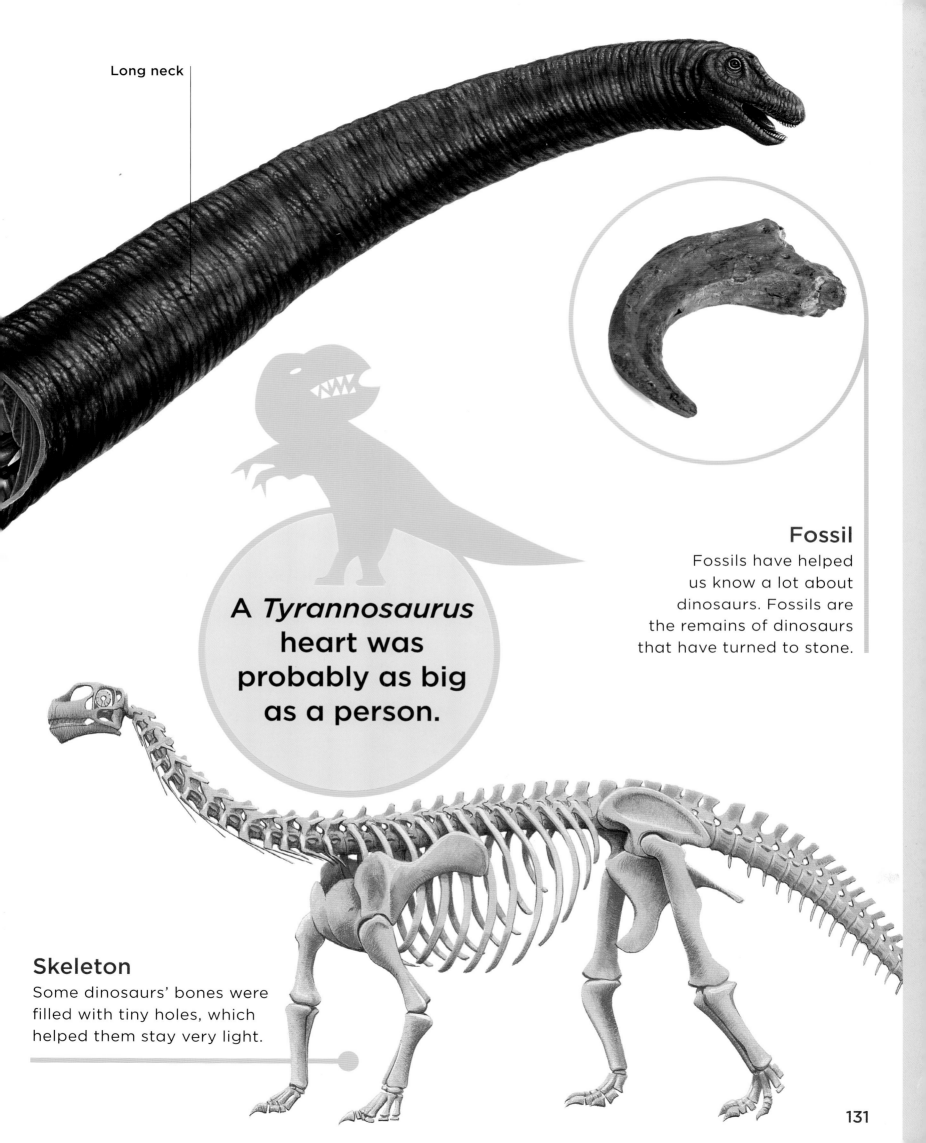

Long neck

Fossil
Fossils have helped us know a lot about dinosaurs. Fossils are the remains of dinosaurs that have turned to stone.

A *Tyrannosaurus* heart was probably as big as a person.

Skeleton
Some dinosaurs' bones were filled with tiny holes, which helped them stay very light.

Meat eaters

Some meat-eating dinosaurs ate prey larger than themselves. Others ate smaller food, such as eggs and insects. Meat-eating dinosaurs all had short, muscular bodies with low, powerful tails, and strong back legs.

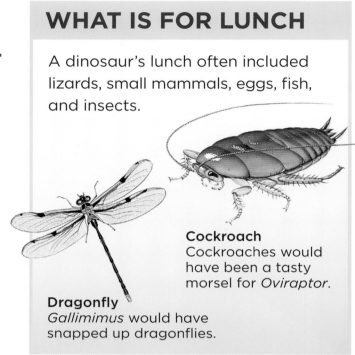
Lunchtime
Dinosaurs used their hands, teeth, or sharp beaks to catch and eat their food.

Hand it to me
Compsognathus liked lizard lunches.

Hooked
Baryonyx enjoyed fish for lunch.

One gulp
Gallimimus snapped up small animals.

Ferocious foe
Deinonychus had long, slashing claws on its back legs, which it used to attack prey.

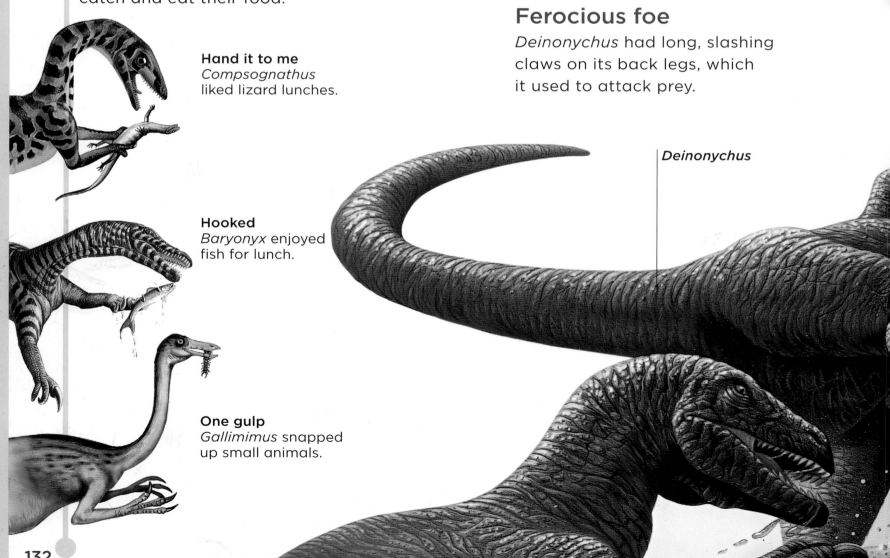

Deinonychus

Tenontosaurus

Spinosaurus was the largest meat-eating dinosaur.

Plant eaters

Plant-eating dinosaurs ate ferns, treetops, pinecones, and flowering plants. Many of them had special cheeks in which they stored the plants while they were chewing. Some had different kinds of teeth for cutting and grinding.

Plant eaters
Plant-eating dinosaurs came in many shapes and sizes.

Heterodontosaurus
This dinosaur may have used its hands to pick up the plants it ate.

There were hundreds of different plant-eating dinosaurs.

Eat up
The plant-eating sauropods were the biggest dinosaurs of all. They had to eat huge quantities of plants to provide them with enough energy to live.

Centrosaurus
The strong jaws of *Centrosaurus* sheared through stems and leaves.

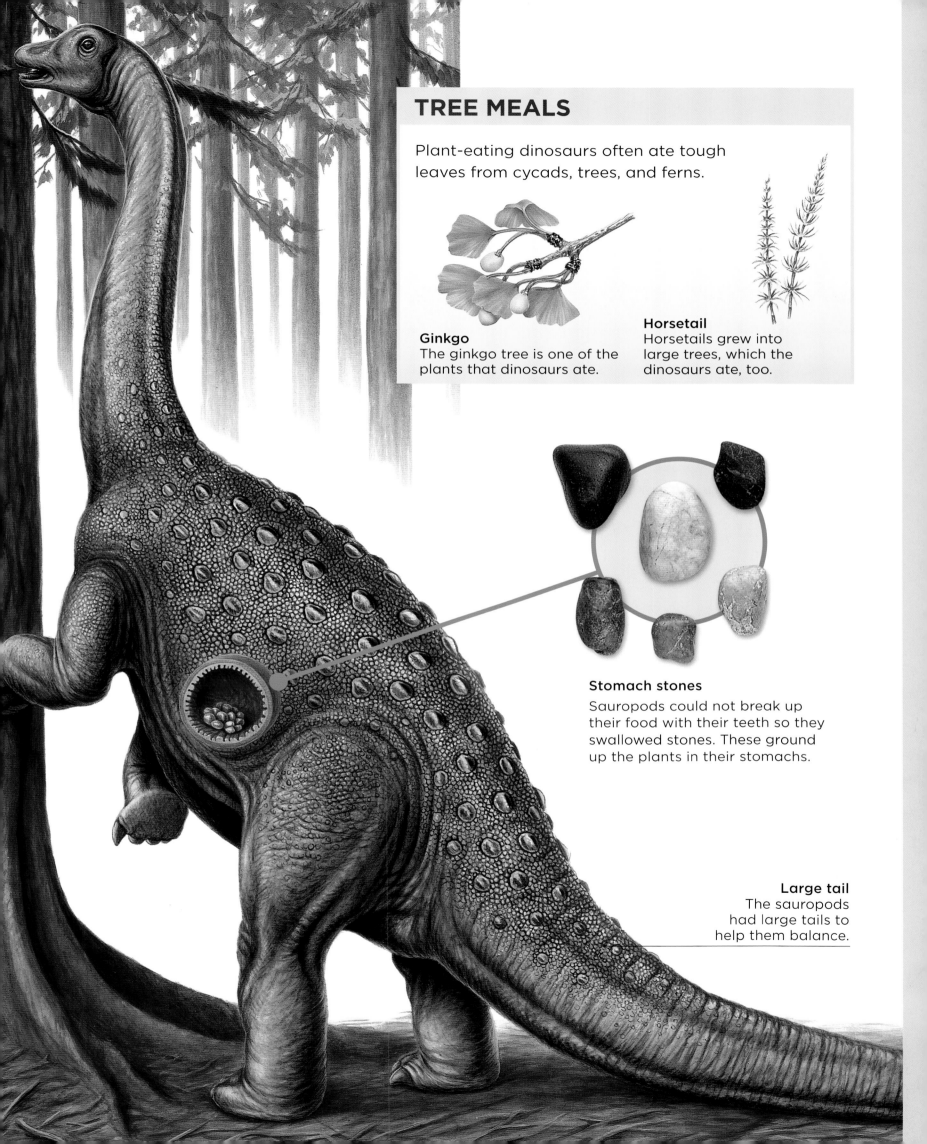

TREE MEALS

Plant-eating dinosaurs often ate tough leaves from cycads, trees, and ferns.

Ginkgo
The ginkgo tree is one of the plants that dinosaurs ate.

Horsetail
Horsetails grew into large trees, which the dinosaurs ate, too.

Stomach stones
Sauropods could not break up their food with their teeth so they swallowed stones. These ground up the plants in their stomachs.

Large tail
The sauropods had large tails to help them balance.

Large and small

Dinosaurs were the biggest, heaviest, and longest land animals that have ever lived. However, there were actually more small dinosaurs than large ones. Here is how some of the biggest and smallest measure up.

Size matters

Three of the biggest dinosaurs that we know of were found in the United States. They were *Supersaurus, Giraffatitan,* and *Seismosaurus.*

Heaviest
The heaviest dinosaur is *Brachiosaurus,* which was as tall as a four-story building.

Longest
Diplodocus is the longest known dinosaur. It used its tail to defend itself against its foes.

Smallest
One of the smallest known dinosaurs is *Compsognathus.*

The longest dinosaur name is *Micropachy-cephalosaurus.*

Biggest?
For many years, *Tyrannosaurus* was known as the largest ever meat eater. Now we know of other, larger ones.

Fast and slow

Fast-moving dinosaurs usually had small, streamlined bodies and long back legs. They could run quickly to escape their larger, more powerful enemies. The big, plant-eating dinosaurs slowly lumbered along, shaking the ground around them as they walked.

The fastest dinosaur would leave the fastest human far behind.

Slow down

Diplodocus and *Apatosaurus* were slow-moving beasts with large bodies and long necks and tails.

Diplodocus

Apatosaurus

You cannot catch me!

Gallimimus could race along at speeds of up to 30 miles per hour (48 km/h). It could change direction suddenly too, so it could easily dodge out of the reach of *Albertosaurus*.

Big and slow

Tyrannosaurus was so big and heavy that it could run only as fast as the fastest human.

139

Attack and defense

Dinosaurs had to fight for their survival. They needed to find enough to eat while making sure they were not eaten themselves. Meat eaters used their claws or teeth to attack their prey. Plant eaters had horns, spikes, armor, or tail clubs for protection.

Camouflage colors

We do not know what colors dinosaurs were. They probably were the same color as their environment to help them hide from enemies.

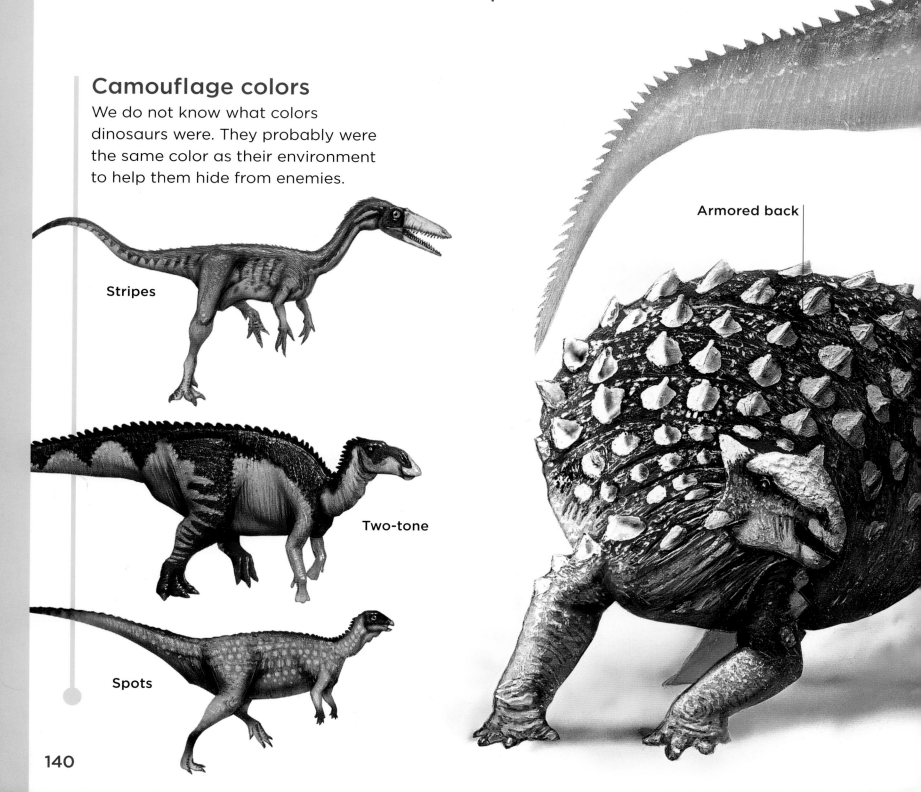

Stripes

Two-tone

Spots

Armored back

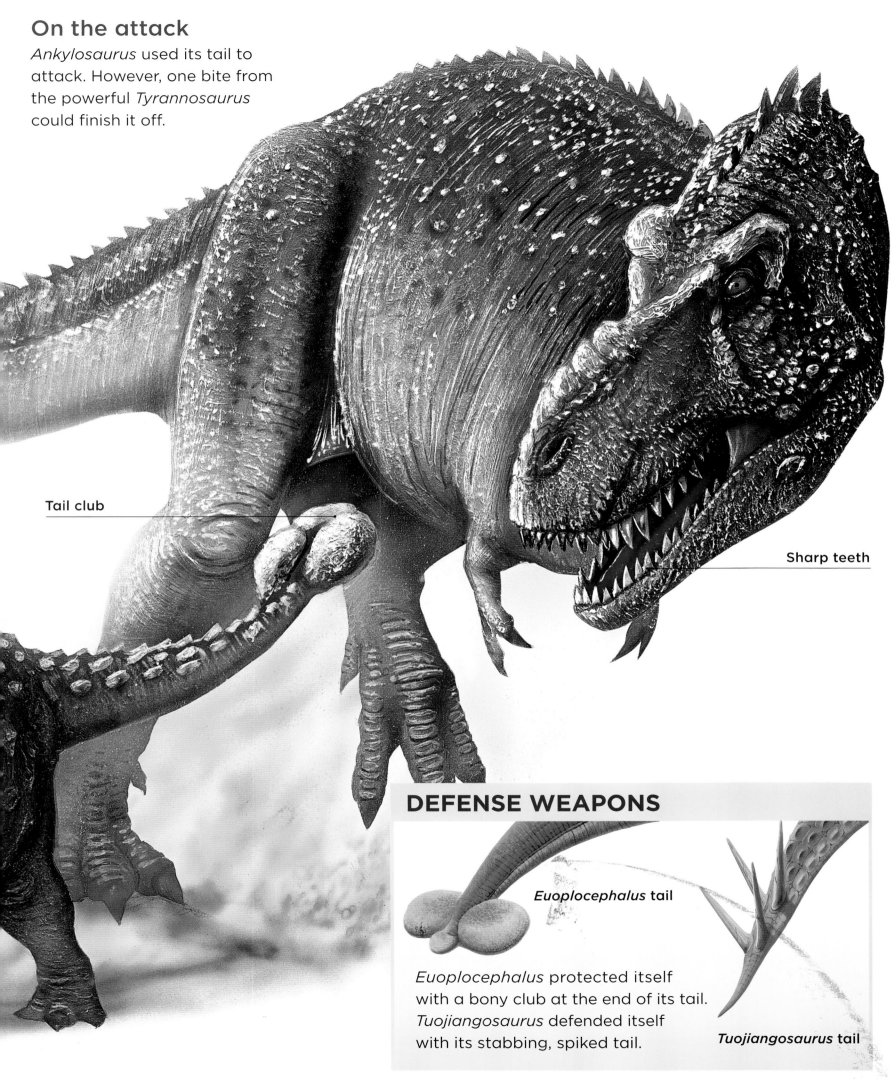

On the attack

Ankylosaurus used its tail to attack. However, one bite from the powerful *Tyrannosaurus* could finish it off.

Tail club

Sharp teeth

DEFENSE WEAPONS

Euoplocephalus tail

Euoplocephalus protected itself with a bony club at the end of its tail. *Tuojiangosaurus* defended itself with its stabbing, spiked tail.

Tuojiangosaurus tail

On the move

Plant-eating dinosaurs often moved in herds to search for fresh food. Some herds had more than 10,000 dinosaurs in them. Meat eaters, such as *Tyrannosaurus*, lurked behind the thundering group, ready to attack any weak or sick animals.

Solitary
Because it lived alone, *Euoplocephalus* defended itself with its bony armor and a club on its tail.

Race against time
A herd of crested *Corythosaurus* and horned *Chasmosaurus* race across a North American plain in search of food.

How do we know?
When dinosaurs walked through mud, they left footprints. Fossils of these footprints show that many dinosaurs traveled in groups.

Moving in large herds was safer than traveling alone.

Dinosaur babies

Dinosaurs laid eggs, built nests, and cared for their young as they hatched. They fed their babies until they were ready to leave the nest. Each dinosaur had its own way of doing things. Most acted more like birds than reptiles when they looked after their young.

The biggest dinosaur egg that has been found is as big as a football!

Dinosaur nursery

Maiasaura nests, scooped out of the mud, contained up to twenty-five hatchlings.

Baby *Oviraptor*

GROWING UP

Here is a one-year-old *Maiasaura* and an adult *Maiasaura*. What differences can you see?

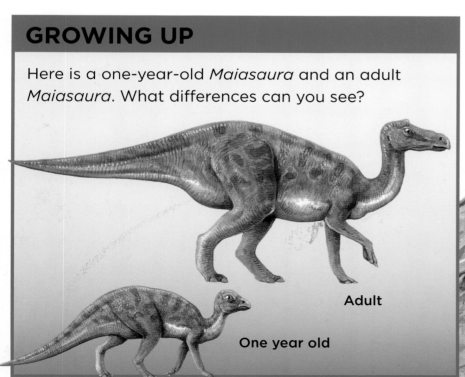

Adult

One year old

Mother
Oviraptor

Feeding time

A mother *Oviraptor*
has freshly killed prey
for her hungry babies.

Sharing their world

While dinosaurs ruled the land, flying reptiles soared through the sky. Long-necked plesiosaurs and dolphin-like ichthyosaurs raced through the seas searching for fish. Turtles and crocodiles swam in the oceans, and early mammals started to appear.

Magnolia

The magnolia is an ancient flowering plant. Plant-eating dinosaurs probably ate them.

NEIGHBORS

Many different creatures lived alongside the ruling dinosaurs.

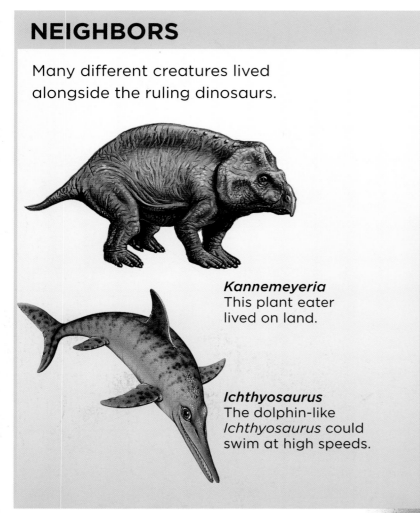

Kannemeyeria
This plant eater lived on land.

Ichthyosaurus
The dolphin-like *Ichthyosaurus* could swim at high speeds.

Swimming
Cryptoclidus swims after a school of fish.

Similar

Some creatures that lived in the time of the dinosaurs look similar to animals that are alive today.

Mammals
Mammals such as this little *Alphadon* lived in the age of the dinosaurs.

Snakes and lizards
Pachyrhachis was one of the earliest known snakes.

Moths and bees
Tiny moths and bees first appeared during the time of the dinosaurs.

Sea and sky

Scaphognathus flies through the air, swooping to catch a meal of fish, while *Cryptoclidus* swims through the water.

Flying
Scaphognathus swoops out of the sky.

Disappearing act

Nobody knows why the dinosaurs disappeared. Some think that a huge meteorite hit Earth, causing dust clouds, acid rain, storms, and huge waves. Others think that many volcanoes erupted and caused the climate to change.

Why did they disappear?

Cold climate
Maybe the climate became too cold for the dinosaurs.

Hot climate
Maybe the climate became too hot for the dinosaurs.

Volcanoes erupted
Maybe many volcanoes erupted and poisoned the atmosphere.

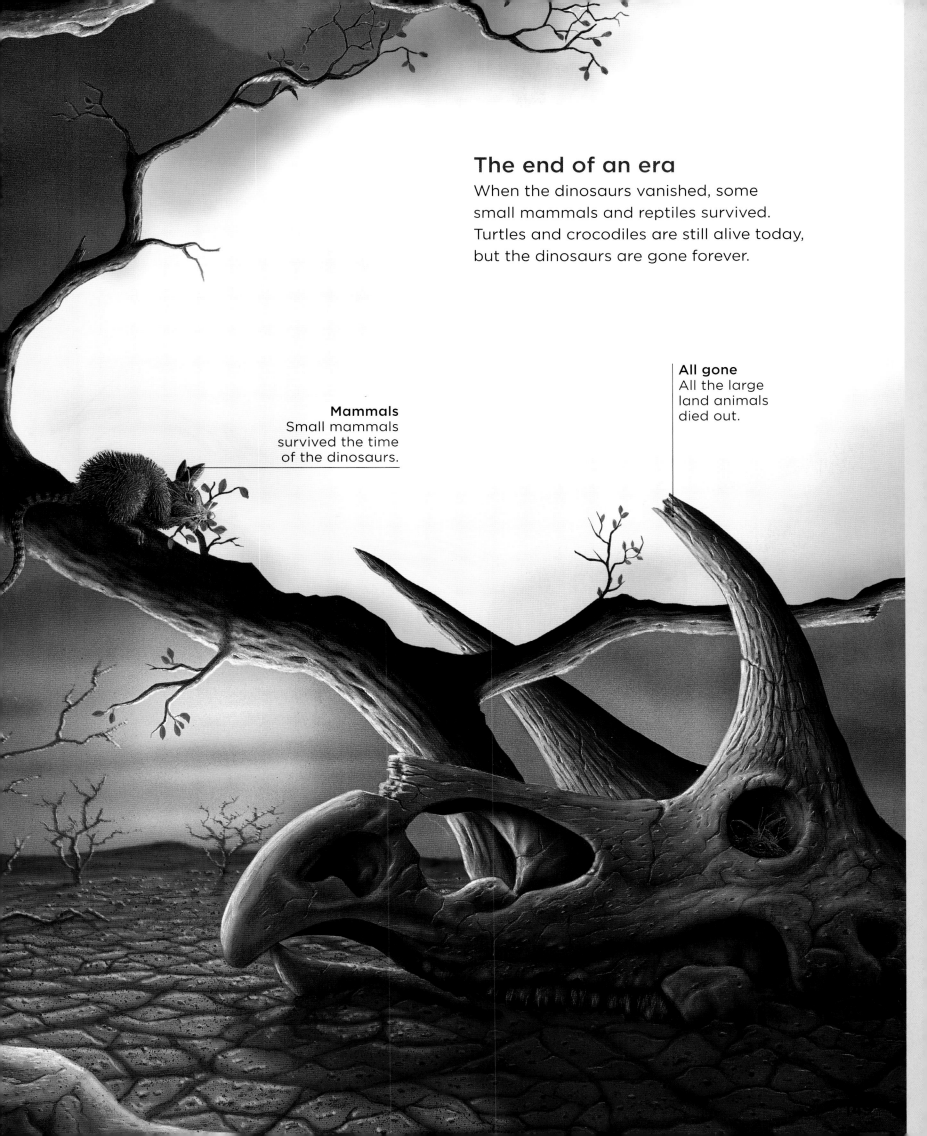

The end of an era

When the dinosaurs vanished, some small mammals and reptiles survived. Turtles and crocodiles are still alive today, but the dinosaurs are gone forever.

All gone
All the large land animals died out.

Mammals
Small mammals survived the time of the dinosaurs.

Great hunters

People who hunt for dinosaur fossils are called paleontologists. They know where to look, and often spend hours searching in places where fossils have been found before. Paleontologists use picks, shovels, trowels, and brushes to uncover the fossils.

Digging carefully

These paleontologists are working on a dig site. Some of them are uncovering the remains of a hadrosaur, while others are making a map of the skeleton.

DOWN IN THE SWAMP

Dozens of dinosaurs died in swamps. The swamps gradually became coal beds and the dinosaur skeletons became fossils. Millions of years later, some of these fossils have been found.

Hide and seek

Fossils can be found in many different types of rock. There are some places on Earth where the rocks are packed full of dinosaur fossils.

Paleontologists

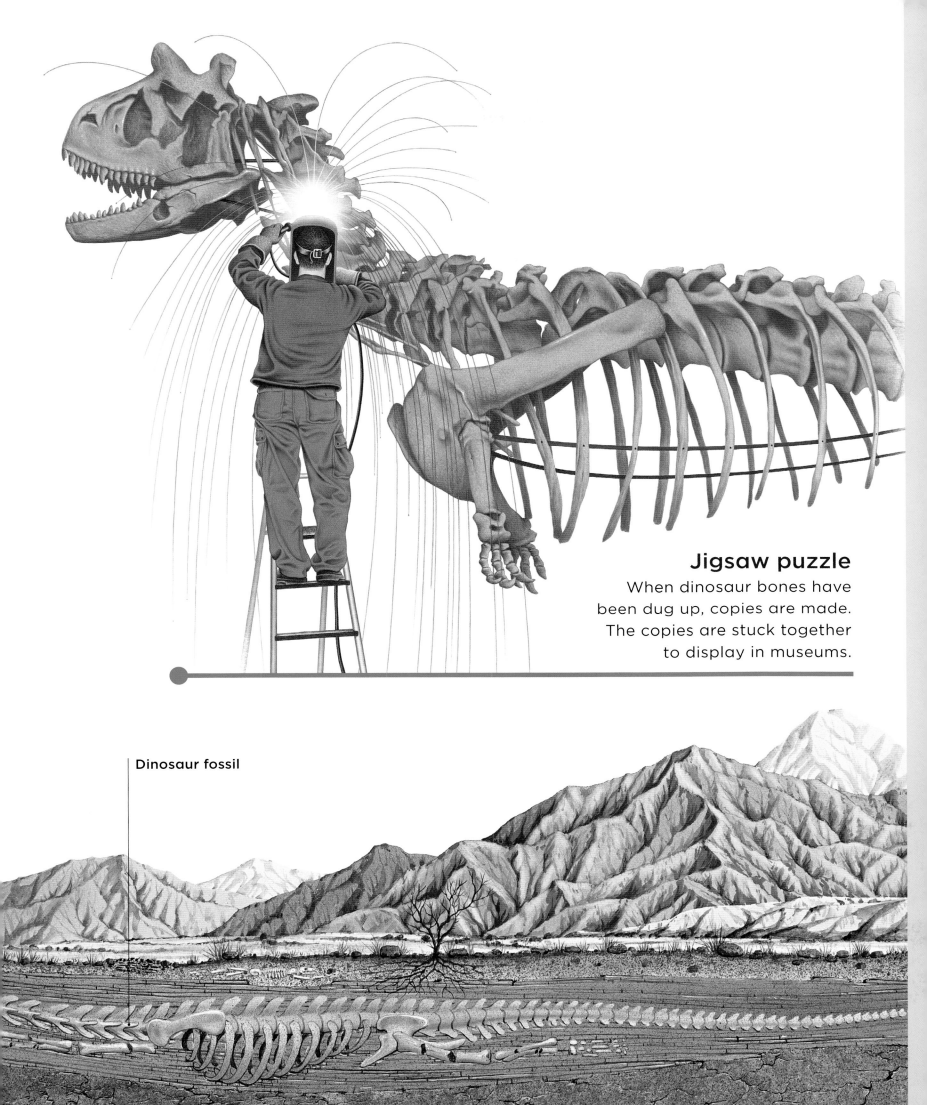

Jigsaw puzzle

When dinosaur bones have been dug up, copies are made. The copies are stuck together to display in museums.

Dinosaur fossil

Archaeopteryx

People did not know if *Archaeopteryx* was a bird or a dinosaur when it was first discovered. Now we know it was a bird that lived alongside the dinosaurs. It had large wings that were covered in feathers, big eyes, and a beak that was filled with small teeth.

The name *Archaeopteryx* means "ancient wing."

Fossil

This fossil shows the feathers and skeleton of *Archaeopteryx*. The fossil is about 150 million years old.

Flying food

Archaeopteryx was a meat eater. It lived near the sea and probably hunted small fish and insects.

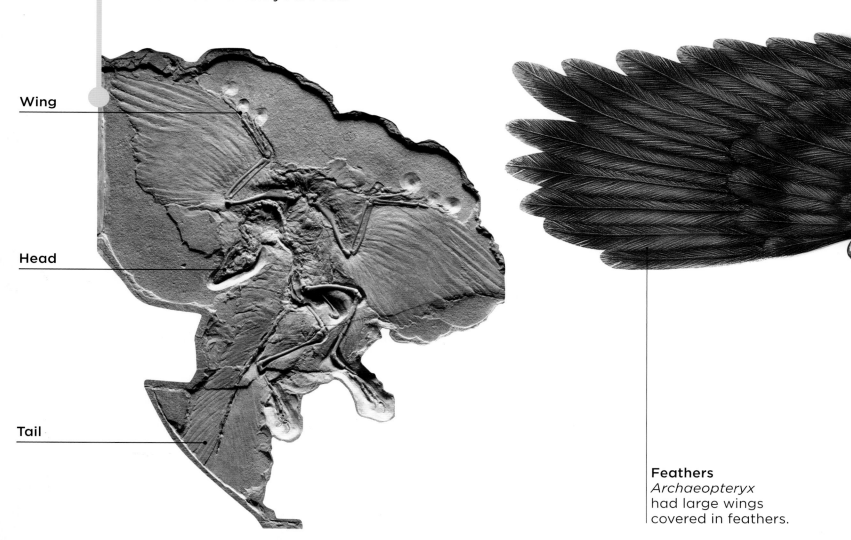

Wing

Head

Tail

Feathers
Archaeopteryx had large wings covered in feathers.

Wing

Food
Archaeopteryx probably ate insects, such as this dragonfly.

WINGS

Birds that live today are related to *Archaeopteryx*. Their wing bones and feathers are almost the same.

Archaeopteryx wing

Pigeon wing

Tyrannosaurus

Tyrannosaurus had strong jaws for crunching through flesh and bone, and a good sense of smell. *Tyrannosaurus* had big back legs, but could not run very quickly. It probably survived on meat it could find from dinosaurs that were already dead.

Huge teeth

Tyrannosaurus had a mouth filled with teeth. Each tooth had rough edges to help it saw through meat and bone.

BIG JAW

Meat-eating dinosaurs, such as *Tyrannosaurus,* had jaws that could open wide so they could swallow large chunks of flesh.

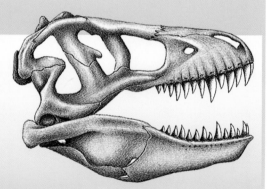

Walking

Tyrannosaurus walked on long back legs. Its front legs were small and had no known use.

Front legs

Tyrannosaurus teeth were as big as bananas!

Open wide

Tyrannosaurus had powerful jaws and large, sharp teeth. If one of its teeth fell out, another would grow to take its place.

Deinonychus

Deinonychus used the three-clawed fingers on its large hands to snatch small prey or wound large animals. *Deinonychus* walked and ran on its outer toes, which had long, sharp claws. Its stiff tail helped *Deinonychus* to change direction suddenly when it was running to catch prey.

The name ***Deinonychus*** means "terrible claw."

Bony rods
If you look carefully at this skeleton you can see the bony rods of its tail.

PACK HUNTER

Deinonychus lived and hunted in packs, much like today's wolves. Its close relative *Velociraptor* also lived in packs. This pack of *Velociraptors* is attacking a *Bactrosaurus*.

No hope
The *Bactrosaurus* is helpless when attacked by a pack.

Acrobat

Deinonychus may have been able to turn in midair while leaping to catch its prey.

Terrible claw

Deinonychus feet each had three sharply clawed toes. The "terrible claw" was on the second toe of each foot. It could swivel around.

Diplodocus

Diplodocus was a large plant-eating dinosaur with a long tail and neck. It could use its tail like a whip to lash at attackers. The head and brain of *Diplodocus* were tiny compared to its body, but its eyes were large and its teeth were long and thin.

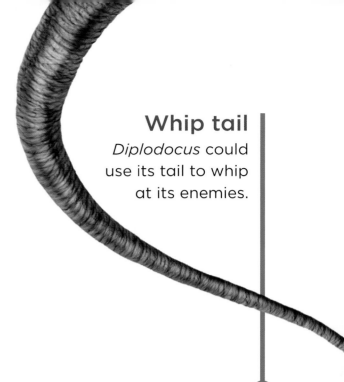

Whip tail
Diplodocus could use its tail to whip at its enemies.

WADING THROUGH WATER

Diplodocus could move through shallow water by floating its heavy body on the surface and moving forward with its front feet.

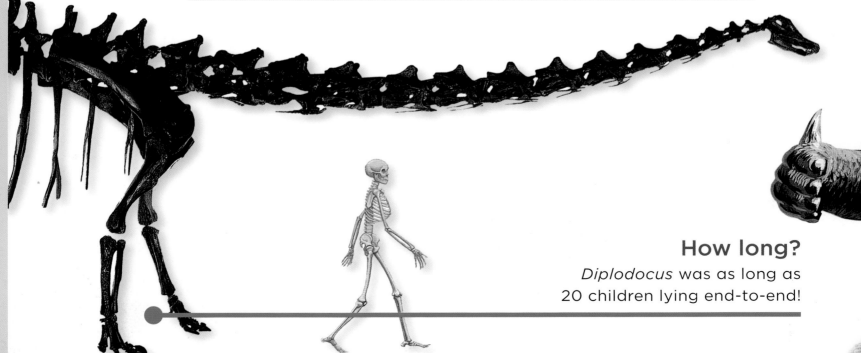

How long?
Diplodocus was as long as 20 children lying end-to-end!

Long neck

Standing tall

Diplodocus could stand up on its back legs to scare away enemies. This also helped it reach leaves on tall trees.

A *Diplodocus* head was the same size as a horse's head.

Stegosaurus

Stegosaurus was a huge dinosaur with heavily built back legs and short front legs. It had flat plates along its backbone, from its neck down to the middle of its tail. *Stegosaurus* had a short head with a long snout and small teeth.

Leg work

The short front legs of *Stegosaurus* helped it to keep its head low, close to the short plants that it ate.

Tail

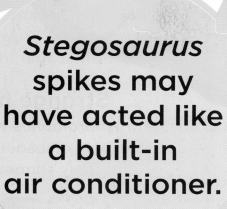

Stegosaurus spikes may have acted like a built-in air conditioner.

Colorful creatures

Stegosaurus may have been colored to blend in with the plants it lived near.

Head down
Stegosaurus kept its head down close to food.

Plant eaters
Stegosaurus ate ferns and other plants.

RELATIVES

Tuojiangosaurus and *Kentrosaurus* are thought to be close relatives of *Stegosaurus*. Can you see how similar they are?

Tuojiangosaurus

Kentrosaurus

Triceratops

Triceratops was a plant-eating dinosaur that traveled around in small groups. Its large, strong body and horned head were similar to that of a rhinoceros. It moved slowly, but it could use its armor of horns and a bony neck frill to fight off attackers.

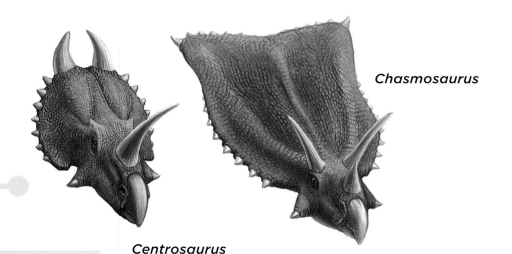

Horn

Charge!

When an enemy attacked, *Triceratops* would charge. Its sharp horns would scare away most attackers.

Chasmosaurus

Head case

Some dinosaurs had head plates. *Chasmosaurus* used its head plate to help it find a mate. *Centrosaurus* used its head plate to fight enemies.

Centrosaurus

ONE OF THE LAST

Triceratops was roaming Earth toward the end of the age of dinosaurs. It was probably one of the last of the dinosaurs.

Bony neck frill

The name *Triceratops* means "three-horned face."

Legs
Triceratops had thick, strong legs.

Glossary

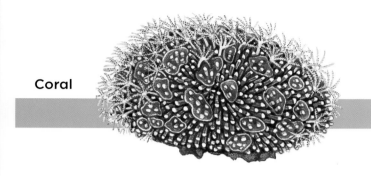
Coral

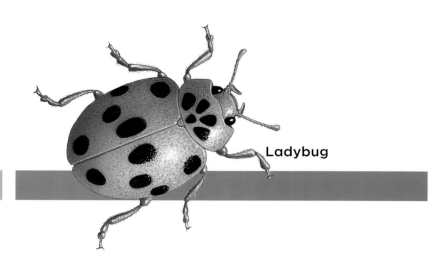
Ladybug

acid rain

Rain that has harmful gases in it

amphibians

Animals with a backbone able to live in water and on land

ancestors

Early peoples to whom we are related

ancient

Existed in times long, long ago

Antarctica

The continent of land, ice, and snow that surrounds the South Pole

antennae

The long growths on the heads of insects, which they use to sense the world around them

aphids

A group of small insects that suck up plant juices

arctic

The region near Earth's North Pole

armor

A covering that keeps something safe

atmosphere

A mixture of gases that surrounds Earth

attacker

An insect or spider that tries to hurt another

baleen

Long strips of an elastic-like substance in the mouths of some kinds of whales

beluga

A white whale with a large, round head that lives in seas near the North Pole

birds

Feathered animals with wings

Dilophosaurus

Arctic tern

chimpanzee

An African ape found in tropical forests

climate

The weather conditions of a place during a full year

continent

A large, unbroken mass of land

coral

A colored substance, formed from the skeletons of tiny sea creatures called coral polyps

creatures

All living insects and animals, other than human beings

crests

Growths at the top of animals' heads

crustacean

A sea creature with a hard outer shell

cycads

An ancient group of seed plants

defend

To protect from danger or attack

delicate

Very fine in texture, such as a spider's web

deliver

To give to another

dew

Drops of moisture

Glossary

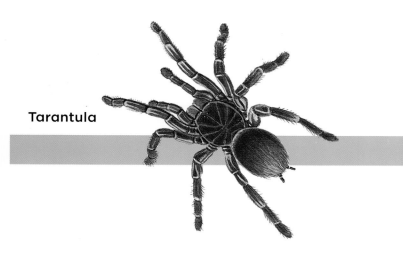

Tarantula

Seal

digesting
Breaking up food so that it can be absorbed into the body

direction
The point toward which something moves

dorsal fin
The fin that appears on the back of a whale or a fish

enemies
Groups of bugs that are violent toward other groups of bugs

environment
The surrounding conditions

Equator
The imaginary line around Earth that divides the top half from the bottom

erupted
Forced out violently

eyelets
The many tiny eyes that make up some insects' eyes

fangs
Long, pointed growths, similar to teeth

fish
Animals that live in the water, and breathe through gills

flare
To spread or curve outward

fleet-footed
Able to move swiftly

foes
Enemies or opponents

gills
Organs on the side of a fish's head through which it breathes oxygen

hadrosaur
A duck-billed dinosaur

Orangutan

Long-beaked
common dolphin

hatchlings
Baby dinosaurs

herds
Groups of animals that live together

ichthyosaurs
Giant sea reptiles

iguana
A type of large lizard that is found mainly in South America

inject
To insert fluid into the body of another, such as a spider injecting venom into its prey

invertebrates
Animals without backbones

joints
Places where two or more body parts join

keratin
A tough protein that forms the outer layer of hair, nails, and horns

krill
Tiny, shrimp-like sea animals

larvae
Small wormlike creatures that hatch from the eggs of insects and some fish

mammals
Animals whose young feed on their mothers' milk

Glossary

Euoplocephalus

Yellow emperor moth

meteorite
A small, solid body from space that reaches Earth's surface

migration
The long journey that many animals, such as birds, whales, and some fish, make from one part of Earth to another

mollusks
A sea creature with a soft body and a hard shell

muscles
Tissues made up of fibers that help bodies move

muzzle
The snout of an animal

nectar
A sugary substance that insects eat

nymph
A baby insect that can sometimes look similar to its parents

ocean
A large area of seawater on Earth's surface. There are five oceans on Earth.

orca
A large black and white dolphin that hunts penguins, fish, and seals

paleontologist
A scientist who studies fossils

plankton
Tiny plants or animals that float or swim slowly through the water

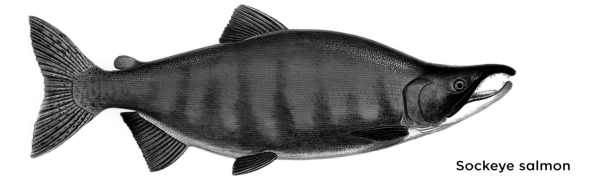

Sockeye salmon

Brown bear

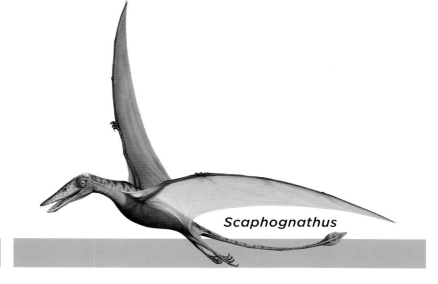

Scaphognathus

plesiosaurs
Flippered sea reptiles with long necks

polar
Areas near Earth's North
and South poles

pouch
A type of pocket used to carry
a marsupial's young

predators
Animals that live by hunting
and feeding on other animals

prey
Any animal hunted or killed
by another animal

protect
To keep or guard from harm

pupa
The stage between larva
and adult in some insects

marmot
A small, burrowing rodent

marsupials
A group of mammals in which the
mother nurses her young in a pouch

Hairy bee fly

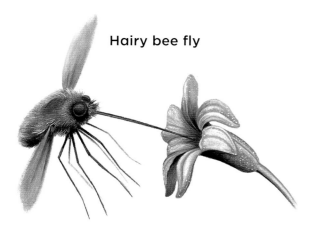

Glossary

Tyrannosaurus

Scarlet macaw

raptors
Birds of prey that hunt for food using their talons

reef
A line of rocks or coral near the surface of the water

reptiles
Cold-blooded, air-breathing animals

ruff
A ring of differently marked hair around the neck of an animal

sauropods
Large, four-legged, plant-eating dinosaurs with long necks and small heads

scales
Thin, flat pieces forming the skin that covers a butterfly's wings

senses
The powers of sight, hearing, smell, taste, and touch

species
A group of animals able to breed among themselves

stalk
To approach quietly and secretly

strands
Single threads, such as those that make up a spider's web

suckers
Parts of the tentacles of an octopus that stick onto fish and other sea creatures

survive
To continue to live

Clownfish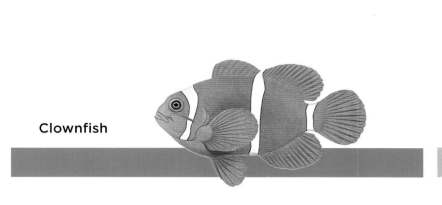

European wasp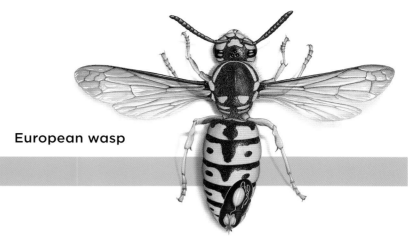

talons

A bird of prey's claws

tentacles

The long, thin outer parts of octopuses and some other sea creatures

theropods

Meat-eating dinosaurs that walked on two legs and had clawed feet

threatened

The possibility that one may be hurt

tilt

To be in a sloping position

tropical

The areas of Earth that are near the equator

tuft

A bunch of hair held tightly at the base

venom

A poison used by stinging or biting insects

venomous

Able to make venom

vertebrates

Animals with a spine or backbone

victim

A bug that suffers injury or death

volcanoes

Breaks in Earth's crust through which gases and lava escape

Index

Credits

Tyrannosaurus

Madagascan sunset moth

Swallowtail butterfly